HOOK
LINE &
SINKER

HOOK LINE & SINKER

An essential guide to New Zealand fish

Daryl Crimp

HarperCollins*Publishers*

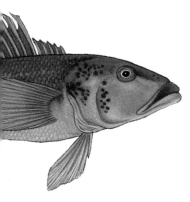

National Library of New Zealand
Cataloguing-in-Publication Data

Crimp, Daryl, 1958-
Hook, line & sinker : an essential guide to
New Zealand fish /
Daryl Crimp.
ISBN 1-86950-473-9
1. Fishing—New Zealand—Guidebooks. 2. Fishes—New
Zealand—Identification. 3. Cookery (Fish) I. Title.
799.10993—dc 21

First published 2003
HarperCollins*Publishers (New Zealand) Limited*
P.O. Box 1, Auckland

Copyright © Daryl Crimp 2003
Illustrations copyright © Helen Casey 2003

Daryl Crimp asserts the moral right to be identified as the
author of this work.

ISBN 1 86950 473 9

Designed and typeset by Richard Wheatley@ Red Design, Auckland
Printed by Brebner Print, Auckland

Contents

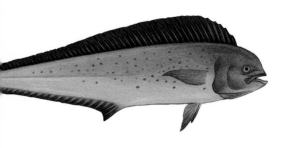

Bait Fish

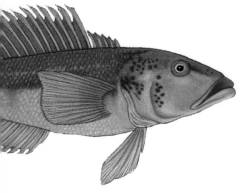

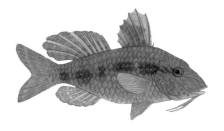

Deep-water Fish

Game Fish

Acknowledgements

This book would not have been possible without the help of the following people: Tony Entwistle, Frank Best, Mike Rendle, John Eichelsheim, Jason Tether, Pete Lamb, Mavis, staff from the Department of Conservation and the Ministry of Fisheries, and the many people who have fed me snippets of information during my forays into the fishing world. If I have misplaced your name, I certainly haven't forgotten what you taught me. No one person knows it all, but it is a great adventure learning just part of it.

Crimpy

Bibliography

R.B. Doogue and J.M. Moreland (1960), *New Zealand Sea Anglers' Guide*, Reed, Auckland.

New Zealand Fishing Industry Board (1981), *Guide Book to New Zealand Commercial Species*, NZFIB, Wellington.

Larry Paul (1986), *New Zealand Fishes: Identification, natural history and fisheries*, Reed, Auckland.

Chris Paulin (1988), *Common New Zealand Marine Fishes*, Canterbury University Press, Christchurch.

www.fish.govt.nz

How to use this book

Recreational fishing is one of the most popular sports in New Zealand. Its beauty is that it discriminates against no one: it can be enjoyed by people of all ages and from all walks of life, and be pursued at any level, be it catching a feed off the rocks or battling a prize game fish in the open ocean.

With the first cast, one begins the never-ending process of acquiring knowledge and skills that bring increasing rewards and fulfilment in the pursuit of the elusive fish. The ability to identify fish and where they live is fundamental to getting the most from the sport and to becoming a better fisher.

This book is designed as a silent companion for when you next add line to water. It does not attempt to cover every species found in New Zealand waters, focusing rather on the most common and popular species — those the recreational fisher is most likely to encounter when fishing the coastal margins. While it can be used as a guide to identifying unfamiliar species that come to your line, it is more than that and can be used in many ways.

The book proceeds species by species. For each, there is an illustration and general description to aid identification, information on habitat and key behavioural patterns to help with the location of likely haunts, and tips on the best techniques to improve the chances of successful targeting. Seasonal movements and availability are noted and take limits listed — daily bag per person, minimum size and, where relevant, minimum set-net mesh. For those who enjoy a taste from the briny, a guide to food qualities is supplied, along with some of my favourite recipes for the best eating species. Unless otherwise stated, recipes cater for four.

While there are many different ways to categorise fish, I've opted for the following simple definitions, as a very basic guide.

 Table Fish are common and popular eating fish.

 Bait Fish are those more commonly caught for use as bait.

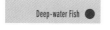 Deep-water Fish are species found in the deeper fringes of our coastal margins.

 Game Fish are those recognised by the International Game Fishing Association as target species for potential records.

Regulations

The management of marine fish is the responsibility of the Ministry of Fisheries. The ministry has divided the country's coastal waters into four main regions — Northern, Central, Challenger and Southern — and a number of subregions. To ensure fish stocks are sustained into the future, the ministry imposes regional bag, size and net mesh limits with regard to some species.

As regulations are tailored to each region or subregion, so restrictions on individual species vary from one place to another. They are also subject to change from time to time. The regulations provided in this book were correct on going to print, but the onus remains on individuals to check local regulations with the ministry before venturing out. The ministry produces pamphlets on the different areas, provides a phone service on 0800 4 RULES (0800 478 537) and operates a website at www.fish.govt.nz.

This book confines itself to listing bag, size and set-net (but not any other kind of net) mesh limits.

Bag limits are of two kinds. The daily per person bag limit is the maximum number of fish of a particular species any angler may take on one day. In conjunction with this, a daily per person combined finfish bag limit applies. Combined bag limits vary with respect to the species specified as well as the numbers that may be taken. Unless stated as separate, the individual species bag limit forms part of the combined finfish bag limit.

Take, for example, the restrictions in Northern concerning tarakihi. The ministry imposes a combined bag limit of 20 finfish. This means you are allowed to take 20 finfish in total, for example 20 tarakihi should you so wish, or, say, 4 blue cod, 6 kahawai and 10 tarakihi if a little variety is what you're after. Either way, 20 is your lot. Unless, that is, you also fancy some snapper, for in Northern you are also entitled to 15 snapper on top of the combined finfish bag limit, except in the subregion known as Snapper Area 1 (SNA1), where 9 snapper is the limit.

Sometimes, however, the bag limit for an individual species is less than the combined finfish bag limit, as in the case of blue cod in the Challenger subregion Cape Farewell east to Marlborough. Here a combined bag limit of 20 finfish applies, but only 3 of those fish may be blue cod. To take any more is illegal, even if your total combined catch is less than 20.

This book does not list the different species covered by each combined finfish bag limit. It is the responsibility of the individual angler to familiarise him- or herself with the relevant species in any given region or subregion.

The minimum size limit is the smallest size of fish you may legally take, and is measured from the tip of the nose to the middle of the V in the tail. Minimum sizes are set to allow fish to mature and complete at least one breeding cycle, so ensuring the continuation of the species.

The minimum set-net mesh limit specifies the smallest mesh you may use in a set net, but it is important to note that minimum mesh sizes for other kinds of netting may also apply and that these must be sought outside these pages.

Bag, size and net mesh limits do not apply to all species. Where there are no limits, you may take as many fish as you like and of whatever size you catch. However, anglers are urged to fish sensibly. We all have a responsibility to help manage the country's fisheries, so take no more than you need. Apply the same philosophy with regard to those species that carry limits, too. Just because you may be allowed to keep 15 snapper, why do so if four will satisfy your needs? In other words, limit your catch rather than catch your limit.

How to use hook and line weight charts

With some but not all of the fish included in this book I have drawn up a chart indicating the commonly used hook sizes, line weights and rigs to catch this particular fish.

The blocks of colour indicate the usual range of hook sizes and line weights, while the solid dot indicates the most common.

Techniques

There are many strategies and techniques for catching the wide variety of fish species that inhabit New Zealand's waters, but it is not the purpose of this book to discuss these at length. Rather, I have included a short section on the most popular methods of targeting each species and the tackle most commonly used, including line weight, hook sizes and type of bait. In addition, for the more commonly targeted species I have provided a quick reference table showing appropriate rigs, line class and hook sizes.

Ledger rig

This is a universal rig suited to catching a host of bottom-feeding fish. It consists of a sinker tied at the bottom of a trace with two or three hooks tied to dropper loops above. The trace is attached to the main line via a swivel. (See diagram.)

Lures

Lures are designed to look like small fish and come in a range of patterns, sizes and colours. They can be trolled behind a boat or cast and retrieved.

Live bait

Many predators can be effectively targeted using live bait. Small fish attached to hooks and allowed to swim freely emit distress signals that attract larger predators.

Stray line

This is a very effective rig for fishing shallow water, particularly when targeting snapper. The hook is tied to the end of a trace, which is attached to the main line via a swivel, and the rig is often fished without a sinker. If large baits are to be used, a second — sliding — hook runs freely on the trace above the fixed main hook. When weight is required to get the bait down, small ball sinkers are run freely on the trace above the hooks. (See diagram.)

Running rig

This is a rig for fishing along the bottom in a strong current or from the shore. The hook is tied to the end of a long trace, which is attached to the main line via a swivel. A sliding sinker is run above the swivel on the main line. (See diagram.)

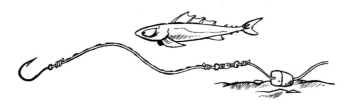

Flasher rigs

These are an adaptation of the standard ledger rig and suitable for targeting bottom-feeding species. The hooks are tied like saltwater flies and designed to resemble small fish or marine creatures such as shrimps. They are best fished with small strips of bait.

Jigs

These are artificial lures designed to resemble small fish. They are dropped to the bottom and bounced up and down to mimic wounded or distressed fish. They can also be retrieved quickly through the lower and middle water column to simulate fleeing prey.

Safety

The pursuit of fish is a tremendous pastime, and the coastline that necklaces New Zealand affords us a fantastic playground, but as in all playgrounds there are inherent dangers.

While the ocean can be incredibly giving, offering up its bounty for us to catch, it can also greedily take from us when our backs are turned. No one plans to drown, but every year fishers are taken by the sea, their loss invariably an outcome that could have been avoided.

An accident such as a drowning is never an isolated incident, but the culmination of a series of events gone wrong. Something as simple as failing to check the weather forecast before venturing out may set in motion a chain reaction that results in a fatal mishap. Careful planning will limit your exposure to risks and ensure the safety of those with you.

Always check the marine weather forecast before you set forth, but never rely on it, as it is only a guide formulated through educated guesswork. Weather at sea can change rapidly and dramatically and be influenced by local geographical features. It is good policy to learn to read local weather signs such as the height, speed and direction of clouds. Watch the horizon for any changes to the ocean's surface and learn to monitor the activity of sea birds. If they are heading for land, so should you.

Have a plan — what are your intentions and estimated return time? — tell it to someone on shore and stick to it. People have often found themselves in dire straits as a result of changing plan and being caught out miles from where people thought they were. It is difficult to be rescued when you are not where you are supposed to be.

If you are going out in a boat, notify the Coastguard of your intentions, the number of people with you and your estimated time of arrival back home. Make sure you have adequate safety equipment for your type of vessel, the kind of fishing you are doing and the area you intend covering. For more detailed information on safety requirements check out www.watersafety.org.nz.

Life jackets, a first-aid kit, flares and a communication device are basic requirements on any vessel. Cellular phones are a handy backup but should not be relied on for several reasons: they may not always be in range, batteries can go flat, salt water may damage them and you can communicate with only one person at a time. A marine radio is by far the wisest choice. It can be heard by whomever is out there, and it allows you to keep abreast of weather updates.

Pack more than enough food and fresh water for the intended journey and carry plenty of spare warm clothing. Make sure that all on board are familiar with the location and operation of any safety equipment, and if you are the skipper, instruct others in the basic operation of the boat.

Fishing from the rocks has become increasingly popular but accounts for a large percentage of annual drownings. Adhering to a few simple rules could save your life:

Safety Checklist

- ☐ Check the weather and tides before venturing out. A rising swell on an incoming tide is bad news.
- ☐ Check the tide margins as some promising locations may be cut off at high tide. Explore unfamiliar areas on an outgoing tide.
- ☐ Study the sea conditions for at least 10 minutes before setting up and avoid rocks that are wet and subject to spray.
- ☐ Avoid fishing alone and preferably fish with someone who is familiar with the area.
- ☐ Never turn your back on the sea as waves come in sets and rogue waves are not uncommon. Have a member of your party watching the sea at all times.
- ☐ Wear warm clothing, nonslip shoes and an inflatable buoyancy vest or light-wet-suit pants. It is good practice to have on hand a flotation aid tied to a rope in case someone falls into the tide.
- ☐ Make sure your equipment includes a first-aid kit, a torch, extra clothing and some form of communication device, such as a marine radio, a cellular phone or flares.
- ☐ Plan a safe time to leave the rocks and stick to it. Hanging on for that last fish may see you stranded by the rising tide.

Whitebait

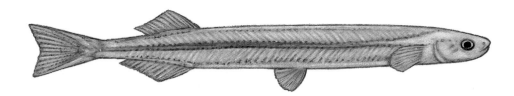

'Whitebait' is the generic term for the juvenile stage of a group of freshwater fish known as galaxiids. Some species have a marine larval phase, and the return to fresh water is referred to as 'the whitebait run'. There are five common species: the inanga, koaro, banded kokopu, giant kokopu and short-jawed kokopu. The inanga is the most common.

As they migrate from the sea, whitebait are small and almost translucent. They are easily identified by their slim profile and large black eyes. The body is light greyish silver, the head small and the tail comparatively large. On inanga, a row of black pinprick dots is visible along each side, as is a row of more silvery dots just above the stomach.

Distribution

Inanga are shoaling fish that inhabit pools, swamps and lagoons inland from tidal estuaries. They spawn in autumn among marginal vegetation during spring tides. The eggs remain high and dry until the following spring tide, when they hatch and the larvae drift out to sea. In spring the larvae commence the famed run back to fresh water.

Inanga are found in pockets around both main islands, but are most abundant on the West Coast of the South Island.

Hook, Line and Sinker

Whitebait are taken in nets during the run. Some people fish the river mouths and surf zones with scoop nets, but it is more common to fish along the riverbanks as the tide pushes in. Scoop nets and set nets are used to trap the fish as they swim against the current.

Food Qualities

Considered a delicacy, whitebait cooks virgin white and has a distinctive if mild flavour. It is best prepared simply, with few accompaniments, as the flavour can easily be masked. It is widely enjoyed in the form of the famed whitebait pattie.

Because of its delicate flavour and texture, whitebait is best eaten fresh. It takes on a slightly sharp flavour when frozen for long periods and loses that subtle flavour, so needs to be double sealed in plastic bags with all the air removed to help maximise its shelf-life.

Whitebait Patties

500 G WHITEBAIT
2 TBSP FLOUR
3 EGGS, SEPARATED
2 TBSP MILK
SALT
CRACKED PEPPER
BUTTER AND OIL FOR FRYING

- Put the flour, egg yolks and milk in a large bowl, season with salt and cracked pepper and blend. Fold in the whitebait.
- In another bowl whisk the egg whites until they are stiff and gently fold into the whitebait mix. This will add air, resulting in light patties.
- Spoon generous amounts of whitebait mix into a pan of hot butter and oil. Cook until light brown on the bottom, flip, and cook for the same time on the other side. Do not overcook, as whitebait dries out and loses flavour.

Seasons

**South Island
West Coast**
1 Sept–14 Nov

Chatham Islands
1 Dec–28/29 Feb

Elsewhere
15 Aug–30 Nov

Tarakihi

The tarakihi is highly prized because of its aggressive fighting nature. It has an oval body, a small head with a tiny mouth, and a forked tail. The flanks are silver and the back is dark grey. A distinctive black saddle draped over the shoulder makes identification a doddle.

Tarakihi will grow to around 60 cm, but 30–40 cm is more common. While a 2–3 kg fish is considered a good catch, specimens of over 5 kg have been taken. Tarakihi are slow-growing and live for about 20 years, although ages of up to 50 have been recorded.

Distribution

Tarakihi are found throughout New Zealand's coastal waters but prefer the cooler climes south of East Cape. There is excellent fishing around Wellington and along the Kapiti Coast. Schooling fish that feed voraciously, tarakihi are commonly caught on the bottom around reefs and foul ground, although larger adults will gather over sandy areas at 100–200 m and tarakihi head for shallow bays at nightfall to feed. Spawning takes place during late summer and autumn.

Hook, Line and Sinker

Focus on reefs and foul ground, both inshore and out to a depth of 100 m. Tarakihi are most active on tides that produce plenty of current, and congregate on the up-current side of obstacles. Use 1–3/0 hooks, small cut baits and shellfish, or baited flasher rigs. Excellent fishing can be had after dark, and tarakihi come readily to berley.

rig	hook sizes											line weight							
	1/0	2/0	3/0	4/0	5/0	6/0	8/0	10/0	12/0	13/0	14/0	2	4	6	8	10	15	24	37
Stray line																			
Ledger rig	●													●					
Running rig																			
Flasher rig	●													●					

Live Bait	Trolling	Spinning	Jigs

Food Qualities

The flesh is firm and white and falls into small flakes. It has a delicate flavour and is suited to all cooking techniques.

Tarakihi Parcels

4 LARGE TARAKIHI FILLETS
OLIVE OIL
1 CUP SLICED MUSHROOMS
2 SPRING ONIONS, FINELY
  CHOPPED
2 TBSP DICED RED CAPSICUM
1 TBSP BUTTER
1 TBSP FLOUR
1 CUP MILK
CRACKED PEPPER
8 SHEETS OF FILO PASTRY
MELTED BUTTER FOR BASTING

- Lightly poach the fillets in water — undercook slightly. Cool and cut into chunks.
- Heat 1 tbsp of olive oil in a pan and sauté the mushrooms, spring onions and capsicum until soft. Melt in the butter and stir in the flour. Pour in the milk, stirring continuously, to make a thick white sauce.
- Add the fish chunks and season with cracked pepper.
- Arrange the filo sheets in two piles of four. Cut these in half so you have four square piles of four. Place a quarter of the fish mixture in the centre of each pile and baste the outside edges with melted butter. Fold the opposite corners of each of the top sheets together and scrunch tight. Fold each of the second, third and fourth sheets in the same way until you have four parcels done up like bonbon wrappers.
- Place the parcels on a greased oven tray. Bake at 200°C for 10 minutes.
- Serve with a side salad and sweet chilli sauce.

Bag limits

North 20
Combined finfish bag: 20
Minimum size: 25 cm
Minimum set-net mesh:
100 mm

Central 20
Combined finfish bag: 20
Minimum size: 25 cm
Minimum set-net mesh:
100 mm

Challenger 20
Combined finfish bag: 20
Minimum size: 25 cm
Minimum set-net mesh:
100 mm

South 15
Combined finfish bag: 30
Minimum size: 25 cm
Minimum set-net mesh:
100 mm

Sea-run Trout

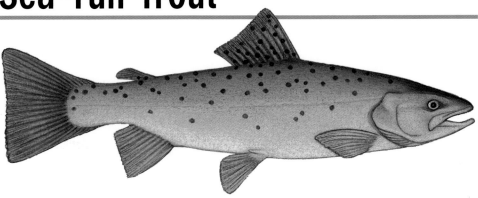

While the brown trout is largely a freshwater species, a percentage of the population migrates to coastal fringes and estuaries. These fish have the characteristic brown-trout shape but are a very distinctive colour, the entire body being bright silver and the body spots muted.

Distribution

Pockets of sea-run trout can be found about the North Island coast south of Auckland, but the heaviest populations are in the South Island. Sea-run trout favour estuarine conditions and will often travel some distance upriver with the incoming tide in search of food.

Hook, Line and Sinker

A specialist approach is usually adopted for taking these splendid battlers. Spring and early summer is the prime season, with dusk and after dark the most productive times of day. While sea-run trout can be taken during any phase of the tide, an outgoing tide is preferred. The fish tend to lie hidden in pools from near the river mouth to some distance upstream, waiting for smelt moving in with the tide. Fly-fishers use wet-fly patterns resembling smelt, casting so the flies drift downstream. The same technique is usually used in estuaries, in pools that have a current flowing through them. The take can be either a subtle touch or an aggressive strike.

Another good time is during the whitebait run, when trout can sometimes be taken by spin-fishers casting very small lures.

Food Qualities

Trout has had a chequered career on the menu, but sea-runs offer a consistent if mild flavour. The flesh ranges from pinkish to ruddy white and is firm and slightly dry. It is best smoked or baked whole.

Fresh herbs such as mint, basil, dill and sage make an ideal accompaniment without detracting from the delicate flavour. When cooking fillets leave the skin on, as it cooks crispy and is full of flavour and nutrition.

Baked Sea-run Trout with Mustard Sauce

Bag limits

1 WHOLE TROUT
75 G BUTTER
4 SPRING ONIONS, FINELY CHOPPED
2 TBSP CHOPPED PARSLEY
SALT AND PEPPER TO TASTE
1 TBSP DIJON MUSTARD
1/2 CUP DRY WHITE WINE
3 TBSP SOUR CREAM
LEMON JUICE

- Melt 25 g of butter in an oven dish and add the spring onions, parsley, salt and pepper. Place the trout on top.
- Mix the mustard and wine and pour them over the trout. Daub the trout with another 25 g of butter. Cover and bake at 220°C for 20 minutes or until just cooked.
- Transfer the hot juices to a frying pan and bring to a simmer, reducing the liquid to about 4 tbsp. Stir in the remaining butter, the sour cream and the lemon juice. Pour this sauce over the trout and serve.

Local river bag limits and seasons apply.

Salmon

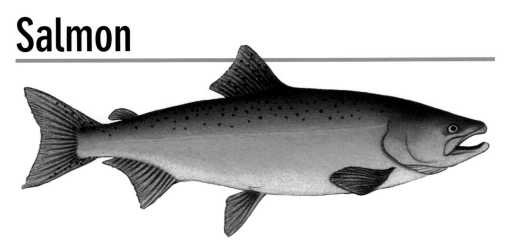

A native of North America, the quinnat — or king salmon — was introduced to New Zealand at the beginning of the 20th century. It has since become a popular target for sports fishers.

The body is elongate and cylindrical, tapering slightly to a broad, triangular tail. It is bright silver, with a greenish tinge and a speckling of small black spots along the back.

It has a single dorsal fin and a small adipose fin on the back. The scales are very small. New Zealand salmon average 50–100 cm in length and 6–10 kg in weight but may reach 25 kg.

Distribution

Salmon are found mainly along the southeast coast of the South Island, although small populations also exist around the Marlborough Sounds, the West Coast and Southland and the odd fish turns up in the lower North Island. They migrate upstream to spawn from late spring to autumn, after which they die, and smolt migrate in the reverse direction about three months later. Salmon spend two to four years at sea before heading back upstream.

Hook, Line and Sinker

Having attained iconic status in the South Island, salmon is a popular target around river mouths and upstream. They do not feed during their spawning migration and are enticed to snap aggressively at lures or spinners cast from the bank and retrieved close to the bottom. Z-spinners and Colorado spoons are popular upriver, while ticers are preferred at river mouths and for sea fishing. Popular colours include silver, silver and red, orange, brass and black.

In some Westland lakes salmon take lures trolled from small boats, while in Otago Harbour they take pilchard baits trolled from boat or cast from the wharf. Common tackle is a 6–8 kg spinning or casting rig.

Food Qualities

Salmon is a superb eating fish. The flesh is pink to orange, firm and flaky and high in oil. It is prized bottled, canned, smoked or baked.

Although salmon is a very forgiving fish, retaining moisture even when over-cooked, it is best served slightly underdone. Mild fresh herbs provide the best accompaniments, along with lemon, lime and orange.

Salmon freezes well but will deteriorate rapidly after three months in the freezer.

Salmon with Yoghurt Dressing

4 SALMON FILLET PORTIONS
250 G LOW FAT NATURAL
  YOGHURT
GRATED ZEST OF HALF A LEMON
2 TBSP LEMON JUICE
1 TBSP FRESH CHOPPED MINT
1 TSP SWEET CHILLI SAUCE
OLIVE OIL
CRACKED PEPPER

• Mix the yoghurt, lemon zest and juice, mint and chilli sauce until well blended and leave to stand for half an hour to allow the flavours to mingle.
• Baste each fillet with olive oil and sprinkle well with cracked pepper. Bake for 10 minutes in an oven preheated to 220°C. Serve with the dressing.

Bag limits

River salmon come under the jurisdiction of local Fish & Game. Foul-hooked salmon are illegal and must be released. Bag limits are separate from combined finfish bag limits.

Central
South Island 2
Minimum size: 30 cm

North Canterbury,
Nelson and
Marlborough 2
Minimum size: none

West Coast
South Island 1
Minimum size: none

Southern 2
Minimum size (Otago Harbour only): 45 cm

Porae

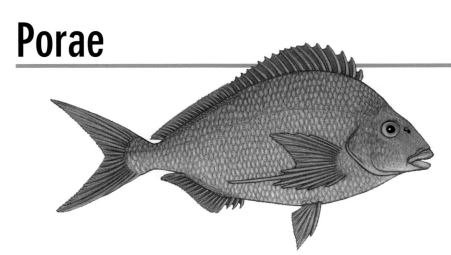

The porae belongs to the morwong family and is similar in shape to the tarakihi, which is also a member. It has a compressed, deep body covered with large scales and coloured greenish blue with a slight yellow sheen.

It has blubbery lips and a large forked tail, and, like the tarakihi, has a long, low dorsal fin and long rays in the pectoral fins.

Porae average 40–50 cm in length but can grow to around 60 cm and weigh up to 5 kg. They are fast-growing when young, but growth slows dramatically once they reach around 40 cm. Porae can live for over 30 years.

Distribution

Porae favour warmer waters from East Cape north, although limited numbers drift as far south as Cook Strait and there have been reports of porae being caught off Kaikoura. They are particularly abundant around the Three Kings Islands. They range in depth from 20 to 100 m and can be found along sandy stretches between and around reefs. They feed largely on small invertebrates in the sand, but will also suck small molluscs from rocks.

Hook, Line and Sinker

Porae tend to be solitary and are therefore hard to target. Fishers usually take them as a by-catch when fishing for tarakihi. They can be taken on the same rig as used for tarakihi, a standard ledger with 1–2/0 hooks, or a brightly coloured tarakihi-style flasher rig. Fresh shellfish baits are best, although cut baits work too. Small blue and white or pink and white jigs are also effective. The porae is a solid fish that will put up a hard fight and is entertaining on light tackle.

rig	hook sizes											line weight							
	1/0	2/0	3/0	4/0	5/0	6/0	8/0	10/0	12/0	13/0	14/0	2	4	6	8	10	15	24	37
Stray line																			
Ledger rig		●														●			
Running rig																			
Flasher rig		●														●			

Live Bait	Trolling	Spinning	Jigs

Food Qualities

The flesh is firm and white and has a delicate flavour not unlike tarakihi. It is suited to all cooking methods, but avoid overcooking as it becomes tough and loses flavour.

Porae in Beer Batter

500–800 G BONELESS FILLETS OF PORAE
1 CUP FLOUR
1/2 TSP SALT
CRACKED OR LEMON PEPPER
1 CAN BEER
1 EGG
OLIVE OIL

• In a bowl, combine the flour and salt with plenty of cracked pepper or a sprinkle of lemon pepper. Gradually add enough beer to form a stiff batter, stirring continuously with a fork, then beat in the egg. The batter should cling to a spoon; if it is too runny, add more flour. Leave to stand for half an hour.
• Dust the fillets with flour and coat with batter. Shallow fry them in olive oil for 3 minutes per side, turning once.

Bag limits

All regions no limit
Minimum size: none
Minimum set-net mesh: 100 mm

Blue Moki

This rather beautiful fish is a member of the trumpeter family and is characterised by its highly aggressive fighting qualities. It has a distinctive small head, fleshy lips, a thin oval body and a pronounced forked tail.

The colour along its back varies from intense blue to blue-grey. Blue moki grow to around 80 cm in length — around 10 kg — and can live for up to 30 years.

Distribution

Blue moki are found right around the New Zealand coastline but are most abundant south of East Cape to a depth of 100 m. They like rocky, weedy terrain but move into sheltered bays in sandy areas between reefs to feed on small crustaceans and molluscs. Adults may be found over more open areas and undertake extensive spawning migrations. Spawning occurs in winter, apparently off the Gisborne coast.

Hook, Line and Sinker

Blue moki are generally taken by shore-based anglers fishing sandy or shingle beaches that lead into reefs and weed. The optimum time for fishing is towards nightfall, when the fish come away from the rocks to feed. They are commonly taken on a ledger rig baited with fresh shellfish or crayfish. They have small mouths, so 1–2/0 hooks are needed.

rig	hook sizes											line weight							
	1/0	2/0	3/0	4/0	5/0	6/0	8/0	10/0	12/0	13/0	14/0	2	4	6	8	10	15	24	37
Stray line																			
Ledger rig		●														●			
Running rig																			
Flasher rig																			

Live Bait	Trolling	Spinning	Jigs

Food Qualities

The flesh is firm and may have a greyish tinge but will whiten on cooking. Blue moki has a strong flavour and is most commonly baked, although it is also suitable for frying and poaching.

Mexican Moki

4–6 BLUE MOKI FILLETS
1 TBSP BUTTER
1 TBSP FLOUR
CAYENNE PEPPER
1–2 CUPS MILK
JUICE AND GRATED ZEST OF A
  LEMON
1 CUP FRESH BREADCRUMBS
1–2 CHILLIES, SEEDED AND DICED
1 TBSP FRESH CHOPPED BASIL
50 G MARGARINE

• Melt the butter and stir in the flour with a pinch of cayenne pepper. Pour the milk in slowly, stirring all the time, to produce a thick sauce. Add the lemon juice.
• Arrange the fillets in a baking dish and pour the sauce over them.
• Mix the breadcrumbs, lemon zest, chillies, basil and margarine. Crumble over the fish and bake at 200°C for 30–40 minutes.

Bag limits

North 20
Combined finfish bag: 20
Minimum size: 40 cm
Minimum set-net mesh: 114 mm

Central 20
Combined finfish bag: 20
Minimum size: 40 cm
Minimum set-net mesh: 114 mm

Challenger 20
Combined finfish bag: 20
Minimum size: 40 cm
Minimum set-net mesh: 114 mm

South 15
Combined finfish bag: 30
Minimum size: 40 cm
Minimum set-net mesh: 114 mm

Blue Cod

The blue cod is not actually a cod but a sand perch. It is distinguished by its large head and long, round, tapering body ending in a blunt tail. Adults are greenish blue, sometimes almost black. Juveniles are lighter, with a brown coloration along the flanks.

Often referred to as rats of the ocean, blue cod do not enjoy an elevated status among sports fishers but can put up a dogged fight on light tackle. They are voracious feeders and will swallow virtually any living organism that isn't nailed down. Size varies depending on location, sex and fishing pressure, with larger fish frequenting South Island waters. Blue cod can grow to over 60 cm long, although but 30–40 cm is more common. They may weigh more than 5 kg, but a catch of 2–3 kg is considered a beauty.

Distribution

Unique to New Zealand waters, blue cod are found right around the coastline, with the heaviest populations south of Cook Strait and around the Chatham Islands. They are territorial, dominant males controlling their own patch, which makes them susceptible to fishing pressure. The Marlborough Sounds, once a prolific blue cod fishery, has suffered a serious decline in numbers over the past decade. Reefs, rocks or foul ground to over 150 m provide suitable habitat.

Hook, Line and Sinker

Because of their aggressive nature, blue cod are easy to catch, often frustrating anglers by attacking baits ahead of more sought-after species. They have a habit of spinning as they take a bait, especially when small, and often leave a rig looking like macramé. The standard two-hook ledger rig, flasher rigs and small jigs are the most preferred tackle. Absolutely any bait will do — even cheese.

rig	hook sizes											line weight							
	1/0	2/0	3/0	4/0	5/0	6/0	8/0	10/0	12/0	13/0	14/0	2	4	6	8	10	15	24	37
Stray line																			
Ledger rig				●										●					
Running rig																			
Flasher rig				●										●					

Live Bait	Trolling	Spinning	Jigs

Food Qualities

The flesh is white to pinkish, flakes easily and has a sweet, delicate flavour. It is superb fresh but doesn't freeze well. Suited to any cooking technique, it is best lightly fried over a moderate heat.

Cod Sticks

500–800 G BLUE COD FILLETS CUT INTO THIN STRIPS
2 TBSP OLIVE OIL
JUICE AND GRATED ZEST OF A LEMON
2 TBSP CHOPPED CORIANDER
2 CLOVES OF CRUSHED GARLIC
1 TSP MINCED GINGER
1 TSP CUMIN OR 1 TBSP ROASTED SESAME SEEDS
PAPRIKA
CRACKED PEPPER

- Blend the oil, lemon juice and zest, coriander, garlic, ginger and cumin or sesame seeds and a pinch of paprika to form a smooth paste. Marinate the fillets in this for an hour.
- Thread the fillets onto bamboo skewers and grill for 2–3 minutes each side, turning once.
- Season with cracked pepper to taste.

Bag limits

North 20
Combined finfish bag: 20
Minimum size: 33 cm
Minimum set-net mesh: 100 mm

Central 20
Combined finfish bag: 20
Minimum size: 33 cm
Minimum set-net mesh: 100 mm

Challenger
Cape Farewell east to Marlborough 3
Combined finfish bag: 20
Minimum size: 30 cm
Minimum set-net mesh: 100 mm

Cape Farewell south to Haast 20
Combined finfish bag: 20
Minimum size: 33 cm
Minimum set-net mesh: 100 mm

South
Southeast 30
Combined finfish bag: 30
Minimum size: 30 cm
Minimum set-net mesh: 100 mm

Kaikoura 10
Minimum size: 30 cm

Southland 30
Combined finfish bag: 30
Minimum size: 33 cm
Minimum set-net mesh: 100 mm

Paterson Inlet, Stewart Island 15
Minimum size: 33 cm

Blue Maomao

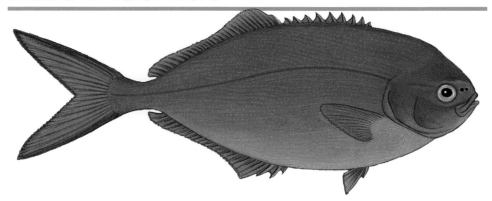

The blue maomao is a member of the drummer family and recognised by its deep, oval shape and laterally compressed body. The head is rounded, the mouth small but flexible and the dorsal fin low and spiny.

It is coloured a uniform iridescent blue with a grey tinge on the leading edges of the tail. It averages 20–30 cm in length but can grow up to 40 cm.

Distribution

Blue maomao frequent mainly North Island waters, usually north of East Cape, although small numbers are found about Cook Strait. Large schools form in the midwater column, where they feed on plankton. Blue maomao are most abundant around islands and reef structures, having a preference for currents and tidal surges.

Hook, Line and Sinker

Blue maomao are not commonly sought by recreational fishers, who usually take them as a by-catch when trying for other small fish. Nevertheless, they can provide entertaining sport on light tackle and bait flasher rigs, small shellfish baits being best, and are attracted by berley. They are also taken by spear-fishers.

Bag limits

All regions no limit
Minimum size: none
Minimum set-net mesh:
100 mm

Food Qualities

The flesh is firm and white, has a medium fat content and makes excellent eating. It has a delicate flavour, which is best enhanced by light frying or grilling.

Greenback Flounder

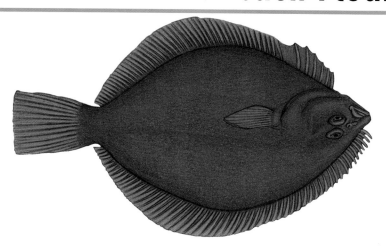

As its name suggests, the greenback flounder is dark green above and white below. It is related to the yellow-belly flounder, and the two are often confused.

Both are oval in shape, but the greenback is distinguished by its pointed snout. Average length is 25–40 cm, but greenbacks can grow to around 50 cm.

Distribution

Greenback flounder are common in South Island coastal waters to a depth of 100 m. They favour sandy habitats and occasionally venture into estuaries.

Hook, Line and Sinker

Greenbacks are most commonly caught in set nets, but can also be taken with dragnets or spears. In estuaries and around river mouths they will also take a line baited with tiny hooks.

Food Qualities

Greenbacks yield nice thick fillets. The flesh is white, moist and delicate in flavour. It suits all cooking methods and is best fresh.

Bag limits

Central/
Challenger 20
Combined finfish bag: 20
Minimum size: 25 cm
Minimum set-net mesh:
100 mm

South 30
Combined finfish bag: 30
Minimum size: 25 cm
Minimum set-net mesh:
100 mm

Trevally

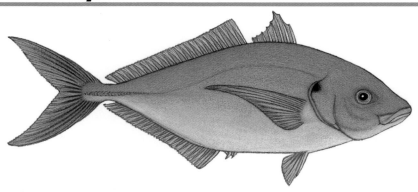

If it's a scrap you're after, look no further than the trevally for some blistering light-tackle action. This slender fish has a blue-green back, often with a hint of yellow, flashy silver flanks and a body that tapers to a distinctive forked tail.

A black mark over the gill plate makes identification easy. Juveniles have a narrower body and distinct vertical bands of green through to yellow along each flank.

Trevally grow to around 70 cm, but 40–50 cm is more common, largely because of the impact of heavy fishing. They can live to over 40 but fish of such age are becoming increasingly rare.

Distribution

Trevally prefer warmer waters so are most common around the northern coast of the North Island, although their range extends as far as the top of the South Island. They frequent a range of habitats, from open waters offshore, where they are often seen working the surface in large schools, and around prominent reefs down to 80 m, to the shallow waters of estuaries and harbours.

Hook, Line and Sinker

Trevally feed on a wide variety of small marine creatures. They are best targeted with small, fresh cut baits or shellfish on 2–4/0 hooks. Most rigs will do, although ledger or flasher rigs are the more usual. Trevally will take small jigs bounced along the bottom, or lures cast into a school when they are surface-feeding.

rig	hook sizes											line weight							
	1/0	2/0	3/0	4/0	5/0	6/0	8/0	10/0	12/0	13/0	14/0	2	4	6	8	10	15	24	37
Stray line				●											●				
Ledger rig				●												●			
Running rig				●												●			
Flasher rig				●												●			

Live Bait	Trolling	Spinning	Jigs

Food Qualities

Trevally is often consigned to the bait bucket but makes superb eating. The flesh is off-putting to some because of its darkish tinge, but it is moist and suited to all cooking techniques. It is ideal baked, although it becomes dry and tough if overdone so is best slightly undercooked at a moderate temperature. It is also particularly good smoked or served raw as sashimi.

Baked Trevally with Oriental Dressing

4 LARGE TREVALLY FILLETS
2 TBSP OLIVE OIL
2 TBSP CHOPPED FRESH LEMON
  GRASS
RIND OF HALF A LEMON CUT
  INTO THIN STRIPS
JUICE OF HALF A LEMON
BLACK PEPPER TO TASTE

• Stir together the oil, lemon grass, rind, juice and pepper in an oven dish. Add the fillets and spoon the mix over them. Cover the dish and bake at 180°C for 15 minutes.
• Place the fillets on a serving platter and drizzle with a little of the Oriental dressing.

Oriental Dressing

1 MEDIUM-SIZED ONION, GRATED
2 TBSP SOY SAUCE
1 TBSP BALSAMIC VINEGAR
1 TSP WASABI PASTE OR HOT
  MUSTARD
4 TSP SESAME OIL
4 TSP OLIVE OIL
2 TSP WATER
CRACKED PEPPER TO TASTE

• Blend the ingredients and chill in the fridge for 30 minutes before serving.

Bag limits

North 20
Combined finfish bag: 20
Minimum size: 25 cm
Minimum set-net mesh:
125 mm

Central 20
Combined finfish bag: 20
Minimum size: 25 cm
Minimum set-net mesh:
100 mm

Challenger 20
Combined finfish bag: 20
Minimum size: 25 cm
Minimum set-net mesh:
100 mm

South 30
Combined finfish bag: 30
Minimum size: 25 cm
Minimum set-net mesh:
100 mm

Yellow-belly Flounder

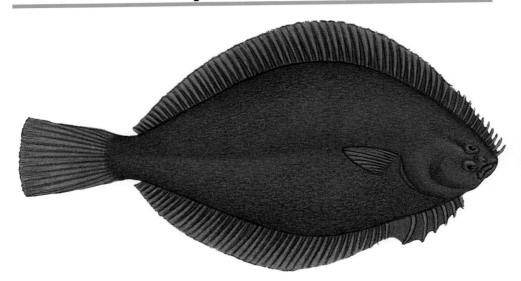

The yellow-belly flounder is similar to the sand flounder but has a narrower oval shape and is dark olive green above and yellow and white below, often with dark spots.

It also has smaller eyes and slightly larger scales than the sand flounder. Yellow-bellies average 25–40 cm in length but can grow to around 45 cm.

Distribution

Yellow-belly flounder are common throughout New Zealand waters down to 50 m. They frequent estuaries, harbours and muddy bays, where their diet consists chiefly of small crabs and other invertebrates. They spawn offshore in winter and spring and migrate inshore for summer and autumn.

Hook, Line and Sinker

Yellow-bellies are commonly taken in estuaries with set nets and by beach seining in bays and harbours and around river mouths. They provide good sport at night for spear-fishers with lights and can also be caught on a rod with small hooks and tiny baits drifted along shallow margins.

Food Qualities

Yellow-belly flounder can be cooked whole or as fillets. The flesh is white and moist and has a fine texture and a mild, delicate flavour. It is best lightly fried, grilled or baked.

Cashew-topped Flounder

FOUR FLOUNDER FILLETS
CRACKED PEPPER
50 G SOFT BUTTER
1/2 CUP CHOPPED CASHEW NUTS
2 TBSP CHOPPED PARSLEY
2 TBSP LIME JUICE
1 TBSP SWEET SHERRY

• Arrange the fillets to lie flat in a greaseproof oven dish, and season with cracked pepper.
• Combine the butter, cashew nuts, parsley, lime juice and sherry in a bowl until blended, then dot generous amounts of the cashew-butter on each fillet.
• Bake at 200°C for 10 minutes. Spoon any remaining pan juices over the fillets before serving.

Bag limits

North 20
Combined finfish bag: 20
Minimum size: 25 cm
Minimum set-net mesh: 114 mm

Central/Challenger 20
Combined finfish bag: 20
Minimum size: 25 cm
Minimum set-net mesh: 100 mm

South 30
Combined finfish bag: 30
Minimum size: 25 cm
Minimum set-net mesh: 100 mm

Sand Flounder

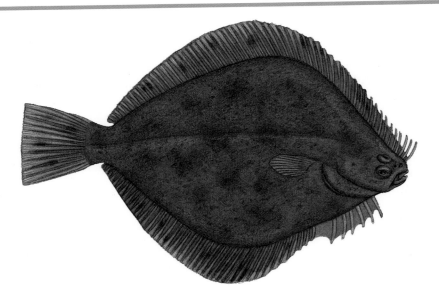

The sand flounder — also known as the diamond flounder or dab — is easily identified by its broad oval to angular shape. It is dark olive green above and white — sometimes greyish and occasionally mottled — below.

The scales are tiny and very smooth. Average length is 25–35 cm with some fish reaching around 45 cm. Sand flounder are fast-growing, females becoming larger than males.

Distribution

Sand flounder are abundant and widespread throughout New Zealand waters, being most prolific around the South Island and in bays of the northern North Island. They range from estuarine areas down to around 100 m, where they feed on bottom-dwelling invertebrates. Spawning takes place during winter and spring.

Hook, Line and Sinker

Sand flounder are most commonly taken in set nets or by beach seining, but are also fun to spear at night under lights. They provide great light-tackle sport when targeted with worms on tiny hooks around the fringes of estuaries. Weight the line with a little split shot 30–40 cm above the hook.

Food Qualities

The flesh is moist, white and delicate. It is suited to all cooking methods but easily overdone. Whole fish and fillets are equally superb.

Like all flatfish, flounder freezes best when left whole. The skin helps to prevent moisture loss and aids the retention of delicate flavours. Fresh herbs such as parsley, basil, dill and sage will complement your flounder.

Sand Flounder with Pesto

4–6 SAND FLOUNDER FILLETS
4 TBSP CHOPPED FRESH SWEET BASIL
1 TBSP PINE NUTS
1 TBSP PARMESAN CHEESE
CRACKED PEPPER
1/4 CUP OLIVE OIL
1 TBSP LEMON JUICE

• To make the pesto, mix the basil, pine nuts and Parmesan in a blender, season with cracked pepper, and gradually stir in the oil and lemon juice until you have a creamy paste.
• Lay the fillets in a baking dish and daub with pesto. Cover and bake at 220°C for 10–15 minutes.

Bag limits

North 20
Combined finfish bag: 20
Minimum size: 23 cm
Minimum set-net mesh: 100 mm

Central/ Challenger 20
Combined finfish bag: 20
Minimum size: 23 cm
Minimum set-net mesh: 100 mm

South 30
Combined finfish bag: 30
Minimum size: 23 cm
Minimum set-net mesh: 100 mm

Common Sole

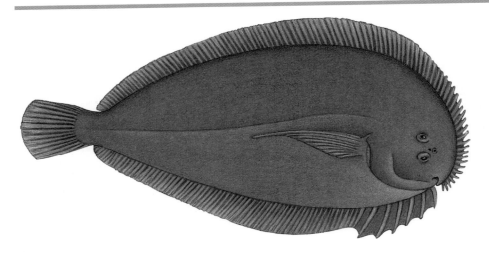

The common sole is oval in shape but not as broad as the lemon sole. It is greenish grey above and white underneath. The head is broad, the snout flat and the mouth hidden by an extended upper jaw.

The eyes are set further back than the lemon sole's and the scales are quite distinct. Average length is 30–40 cm but some fish grow to 55 cm.

Distribution

The common sole is widely distributed throughout New Zealand coastal waters down to 100 m but is most prolific in the south. It is found on flat bottoms in wide bays and sheltered inshore areas, where it feeds on marine worms, brittle-stars and small crustaceans.

Hook, Line and Sinker

Common sole are usually taken in set nets or by beach seining. They can also be speared at night in shallow bays.

Food Qualities

The flesh of the common sole is considered a delicacy. It is white, although the upper fillets appear darker than the lower. Texture and flavour are delicate and suited to all cooking methods, especially baking (whole), grilling and frying.

Baked Bacon Sole

1 WHOLE SOLE PER PERSON
1 BACON RASHER PER SOLE, CHOPPED AND COOKED
1 FINELY DICED TOMATO PER SOLE
1 HANDFUL CHOPPED BASIL PER SOLE
CRACKED PEPPER

• Cut the top skin of each sole diagonally in both directions and place the fish on a piece of foil.
• Top with the bacon, tomato, basil and a good dose of cracked pepper.
• Seal the foil and bake for 15 minutes in an oven preheated to 220°C.

Bag limits

North 20
Combined finfish bag: 20
Minimum size: 25 cm
Minimum set-net mesh: 114 mm

Central/ Challenger 20
Combined finfish bag: 20
Minimum size: 25 cm
Minimum set-net mesh: 100 mm

South 30
Combined finfish bag: 30
Minimum size 25 cm
Minimum set-net mesh: 100 mm

Lemon Sole

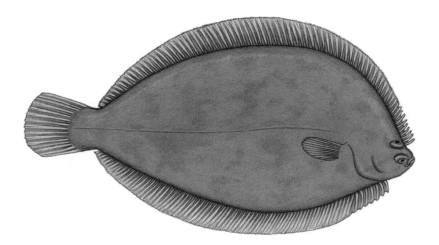

The lemon sole is oval in shape and widest well forward, towards the head, which is small. The eyes sit close to the edge of a slightly protruding snout. The upper body is grey or brown and faintly marbled, while the underneath is white. Average length is 25–35 cm, although some specimens grow to around 50 cm.

Distribution

The lemon sole is found throughout New Zealand's coastal waters down to 100 m, but is more common around the South Island, particularly Tasman Bay, Pegasus Bay and Otago. It prefers flat, sandy bottoms, where it feeds largely on marine worms and brittle-stars.

Hook, Line and Sinker

Lemon sole are occasionally taken by beach seine or in set nets as they drift into shallower waters. They are sometimes taken in scallop dredges and occasionally by spear-fishers.

Food Qualities

The flesh is white with a delicate texture and suited to all cooking methods, especially grilling. Large fish can be filleted but are sweeter cooked on the bone.

Grilled Lemon Sole with Lemon Butter

4 WHOLE LEMON SOLE
50 G SOFTENED BUTTER
$^{1}/_{2}$ FINELY DICED RED CAPSICUM
LEMON PEPPER SEASONING

- Mix the butter and capsicum with a good sprinkling of lemon pepper seasoning.
- Cut the top skin of each sole diagonally in both directions to form diamond-shaped cuts.
- Daub each sole with the butter mixture and grill for 5 minutes, turning once.

Bag limits

North 20
Combined finfish bag: 20
Minimum size: 25 cm
Minimum set-net mesh: 114 mm

Central/Challenger 20
Combined finfish bag: 20
Minimum size: 25 cm
Minimum set-net mesh: 100 mm

South 30
Combined finfish bag: 30
Minimum size: 25 cm
Minimum set-net mesh: 100 mm

Butterfish

The butterfish — also known as greenbone — is long and slender. Colour can vary with age and between the sexes. Young fish are a yellowish brown with white markings along the side. Older fish are generally a dark greenish brown, although large adults may be bluish green to almost black.

The dorsal fin is long and sail-like, and the anal fin is also very long. Butterfish have small 'parrot-beak' mouths and can grow to around 70 cm in length, although they commonly average 40–50cm. They start life as females and change sex as they grow older.

Distribution

The butterfish is common throughout New Zealand waters but increases in abundance to the south. It is a weed-dwelling fish, confined in habitat to shallow rocky areas along inshore coastal margins down to around 15 m. It eats mainly weed, but also small worms and crustaceans. Males tend to be territorial, and populations can be affected by heavy fishing pressure.

Hook, Line and Sinker

Butterfish are most commonly caught with set nets strung across weedy patches close to shore or by divers with spear guns.

Food Qualities

Butterfish causes fishers' taste buds to drool. A prime table fish, it has a firm, delicate flesh high in iodine. It is suited to all cooking techniques, particularly baking.

Butterfish Pie

500 G BUTTERFISH FILLETS
1 CUP MILK
1/2 CUP WATER
SALT AND PEPPER
4 EGGS
CURRY POWDER
SUGAR
1 TBSP OLIVE OIL
1 ONION, SLICED
50 G BUTTER
1/2 CUP FLOUR
5 MEDIUM POTATOES
1 CUP GRATED TASTY CHEESE

- Place the fillets in a saucepan, cover with the milk and water and season with salt and pepper. Poach gently until cooked.
- Strain and reserve the liquid. Place the fish in an ovenproof dish.
- Hard-boil and shell the eggs, dust with curry powder and sugar, then chop and sprinkle over the fish.
- Heat the oil in a saucepan and sauté the onion until soft, then layer it over the fillets.
- In the same pan, heat the butter and stir in the flour. Gradually pour in the reserved liquid, stirring continuously until the mixture thickens, then pour it over the fish.
- Boil the potatoes and mash them with a knob of butter. Mix in the cheese with a fork. Spread over the top of the fish and bake for 15 minutes in an oven preheated to 200°C.

Bag limits

 North 20
Combined finfish bag: 20
Minimum size: 35 cm
Minimum set-net mesh: 108 mm

Central 20
Combined finfish bag: 20
Minimum size: 35 cm
Minimum set-net mesh: 108 mm

Challenger 20
Combined finfish bag: 20
Minimum size: 35 cm
Minimum set-net mesh: 108 mm

South 15
Combined finfish bag: 30
Minimum size: 35 cm
Minimum set-net mesh: 108 mm

Monkfish

The monkfish is the most popular of six species of stargazer found in New Zealand waters. Stargazers are probably so-named because of their eyes, which, protruding from the top of the head, are all that remain visible when these fish bury themselves in silt to ambush passing prey.

The monkfish is a mottled olive brown above and white underneath. The body tapers from the thick, flattish head, the mouth is angled upwards, and a prominent spine points backwards from the base of the pectoral spines. Monkfish average 30–50 cm in length but can grow to 60 cm.

Distribution

Stargazers are common throughout New Zealand's coastal waters but most prolific about the lower South Island. They range from shallow inshore water and estuaries down to around 600 m.

Hook, Line and Sinker

Because of their habit of burying themselves to ambush small fish as they pass, stargazers are seldom taken by recreational anglers. While they are occasionally caught in dragnets they are more commonly picked up in flounder set nets in estuaries. Spearing at night for flounder can also deliver the occasional stargazer to the table.

Food Qualities

Commonly held in low regard as a table fish, monkfish is frequently discarded. Yet it is also referred to as 'poor man's crayfish', and for good reason. The flesh is pearly white, firm and moist, and has a delicate crayfish flavour. The thick fillets are suited to all cooking methods.

Baked Monkfish

4 MONKFISH FILLETS
$1/2$ RED ONION, SLICED
1 TBSP CAPERS
$1/2$ CUP WHIPPED CREAM
2 EGGS, LIGHTLY BEATEN
2 TBSP CHOPPED FRESH DILL
1 TBSP LEMON JUICE

• Place the fillets flat in a greased shallow baking dish.
• Sauté the onion in a pan until soft and stir in the capers. Remove from the heat and blend in the cream, eggs, dill and lemon juice.
• Pour the mixture over the fillets, cover, and bake at 180°C for 30 minutes or until cooked.

Bag limits

 South 30
Combined finfish bag: 30
Minimum size: none
Minimum set-net mesh:
100 mm

Other regions
no limit
Minimum size: none
Minimum set-net mesh:
100 mm

John Dory

You can't mistake a John Dory. Its distinguishing features are a deep, compressed body, a smooth skin, a high-riding dorsal fin and a prominent 'thumbprint' in the middle of each flank.

Its muted olive-brown colour makes effective camouflage, and its large mouth extends like a tube to ensnare its prey.

John Dory can grow to around 60 cm in length. They are fast-growing and can live for up to nine years.

Distribution

John Dory are found in most New Zealand waters but are most abundant north of the Bay of Plenty. There are sizeable populations in Tasman and Golden Bays and around the outer Marlborough Sounds. They frequent a range of habitats from open bottoms down to 150 m to inshore reefs and harbours. The John Dory is a predator that slowly stalks other small fish.

Hook, Line and Sinker

John Dory are targeted primarily with small live baits but will take cut baits, flasher rigs and small jigs. A single-hook ledger rig tied with a long dropper loop and armed with a 3–5/0 hook will do the trick. The live bait is generally hooked through the lip, but some prefer to run the hook through the tail.

rig	hook sizes											line weight							
	1/0	2/0	3/0	4/0	5/0	6/0	8/0	10/0	12/0	13/0	14/0	2	4	6	8	10	15	24	37
Stray line																			
Ledger rig				●											●				
Running rig			●												●				
Flasher rig				●											●				

Live Bait	Trolling	Spinning	Jigs

Food Qualities

John Dory is a superb table fish, yielding firm fillets with a delicate flavour. It is suited to all cooking methods but is best pan-fried or lightly grilled and should be eaten fresh as it doesn't freeze well.

Pan-fried John Dory with Champagne Sauce

4 MEDIUM-SIZED JOHN DORY
  FILLETS
BUTTER
OLIVE OIL
1 1/2 GLASSES BUBBLY
1 TBSP MILD MUSTARD
200 ML DESSERT CREAM
6 THIN STRIPS OF LEMON RIND
CRACKED PEPPER
CHOPPED CHIVES
EGG YOLK

- Heat equal quantities of butter and olive oil in a heavy-bottomed pan. Fry the fillets until just cooked, turning once, then remove them to a warmer.
- Add the bubbly to the pan, stirring any residue from the base, and bring to the boil. Stir in the mustard until well blended, then add the cream, taking care not to boil it. Add the rind and pepper to taste and simmer gently to reduce the liquid to the desired consistency. Pour the sauce over the warm fillets, sprinkle chives on top and serve.
- For a silky sauce, remove the sauce from the heat before it becomes too thick and whisk in an egg yolk.

Bag limits

◣ **North 20**
Combined finfish bag: 20
Minimum size: none
Minimum set-net mesh:
100 mm

◗ **Central/ Challenger 20**
Combined finfish bag: 20
Minimum size: none
Minimum set-net mesh:
100 mm

Leatherjacket

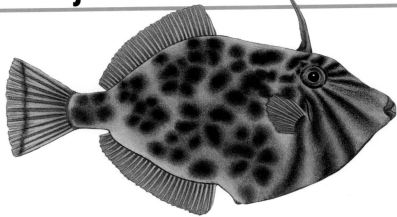

The leatherjacket is easily distinguished by its unusual oval–diamond shape, its compressed body and the folding dorsal spine above its head. It is greyish brown in colour, males uniformly so, females often being mottled.

The eyes are large and set high in the head, which tapers to a tiny 'parrot-beak' mouth. The skin has a sandpaper-like texture.

Leatherjackets are slow-moving and appear to hover when swimming. They usually grow to 20–30 cm long, occasionally up to 40 cm, and live for six or seven years.

Distribution

Leatherjackets are widespread throughout New Zealand's coastal waters. They favour rocky, weedy terrain, usually in the shallower margins down to 30 m, although they have been found at depths of up to 100 m, sometimes over quite open bottoms. They feed on a variety of small crustaceans when young, then take to grazing on algae, sponges and barnacles.

Bag limits

All regions no limit
Minimum size: none
Minimum set-net mesh:
100 mm

Hook, Line and Sinker

Leatherjackets are taken almost exclusively as by-catch and can frustrate fishers by stealing bait. Having very small mouths they must be targeted with tiny hooks and morsels of fresh bait or with small flasher rigs. They are often caught in nets set around reefs and weed banks.

Food Qualities

Sold commercially as creamfish, leatherjackets have a firm, textured, white flesh with a sweet taste, suited to all cooking methods.

Parore

Also known as blackfish, black snapper, black bream and mangrove fish, the parore has a deep body that is dark brown to blackish grey above and lighter, with darker vertical bands, along the flanks. The mouth and head are small. Parore average 30–40 cm in length but can grow to around 60 cm.

Distribution

Parore are warm-water fish, found about the upper North Island. They occupy a range of habitats, from estuaries and mangroves to rocky coastal stretches, where they feed amid white water and heavy surges. They are largely herbivorous, dining on algae and weed, but will also eat small crustaceans and other tiny animals.

Hook, Line and Sinker

Parore are most active around morning and evening change of light. Specialist tackle is required to catch them. A tiny hook (10–12/0) is best, tied at the end of a long, lightly weighted trace attached to a float to keep the bait just off the bottom. Split shot crimped to the trace about 50 cm above the hook will allow the bait to drift naturally with the current to these cautious feeders. Small shellfish baits or fresh strips of seaweed offer the best chance of success. Parore are also taken by spear-fishers or in set nets.

Bag limits

All regions no limit
Minimum size: none
Minimum set-net mesh:
100 mm

Food Qualities

Parore have a medium-firm flesh that is low in fat, which can dry out if overcooked. The gut is high in iodine, which can taint the flesh if they are not filleted immediately. The delicately flavoured flesh is best cooked lightly over a moderate heat. Suitable for frying, grilling and baking.

Spiny Dogfish

Anglers generally consider this dude a nuisance. Two sharp spines protrude from the front base of each dorsal fin, and while these are not poisonous they can deliver a painful wound if care is not taken during handling.

A member of the shark family, the spiny dogfish is brownish grey above, with a spattering of white spots along the back, and almost white below. The top fin on the tail has a black edging. Average length is around a metre, and weight 3–4 kg.

Distribution

Spiny dogfish are most common around the south and east coasts of the South Island. The lower North Island is the northern limit of their range. They frequent inshore waters down to 700 m, are a schooling species and enjoy a varied diet of fish, squid and other invertebrates. The distinct northern spiny dogfish, which lacks white spots, is common in North Island waters between 100 and 250 m.

Hook, Line and Sinker

Spiny dogs are a common by-catch. They will scoff any bait and are commonly caught on ledger rigs on the bottom. If they are present, use large recurve hooks as these are easy to remove. Spiny dogs put up a dogged, jerky fight — nothing spectacular. They are also taken in set nets, often twisting themselves into an almighty tangle.

rig	hook sizes											line weight							
	1/0	2/0	3/0	4/0	5/0	6/0	8/0	10/0	12/0	13/0	14/0	2	4	6	8	10	15	24	37
Stray line					●									●					
Ledger rig					●	●								●					
Running rig					●											●			
Flasher rig					●									●					

Live Bait	Trolling	Spinning	Jigs

Food Qualities

Contrary to common belief, spiny dogfish are perfectly fine to eat. The moist flesh is firm and white, with a mild flavour. Sometimes sold commercially for fish and chips, it suits all cooking techniques and cooks better after freezing.

Spiny Dog Kebabs with Satay Sauce

500 G SPINY DOG FILLETS
SALT
CRACKED PEPPER
2 TBSP OLIVE OIL
BAMBOO SKEWERS

- Cut fillets into 2 cm cubes and place in a dish. Season with salt and cracked pepper and stir in olive oil until the fish is coated.
- Thread 4–6 cubes onto skewers.
- Place under the grill and cook for 10 minutes or until just cooked, turning once.
- Serve on a bed of steamed rice and top with satay sauce.

Satay Sauce

OIL
1 ONION, FINELY DICED
2 TSP MINCED GARLIC
1 TSP MINCED GINGER
1–2 TSP SWEET CHILLI SAUCE
1 TSP CORIANDER
1 TSP CUMIN
1 CUP PEANUT BUTTER
1/2 CUP WATER
1/2 TIN COCONUT CREAM
LEMON JUICE

- Heat oil in a large frypan and sauté onions until soft. Add garlic, ginger and chilli sauce and stir until well mixed. Stir in spices.
- Stir in peanut butter with water and blend well. Add coconut cream and bring to a simmer, stirring until reduced to a thick creamy consistency. Squeeze in lemon juice and simmer for a further minute.
- This sauce can be made in advance and stored for several days in the fridge if necessary.

Bag limits

⬥ North/Central/ Challenger no limit

Minimum size: none
Minimum set-net mesh: 100 mm

⬥ South 15

Minimum size: none
Minimum set-net mesh: 100 mm

Rig

A cat with many hats, rig is also known as spotted dogfish, gummy shark, smooth hound, pioke and lemon fish. It has a slender, sharklike body that is pale golden brown above and covered with a myriad blue and white spots.

It is easily distinguished from the spiny dogfish, with which it might otherwise be confused, by the absence of spines at the base of the dorsal fins. Average length is 80–100 cm and weight 2–4 kg, but rig can grow to around 140 cm.

Distribution

Rig are common throughout New Zealand's coastal waters to around 200 m. Adults migrate inshore during spring and summer, when they frequent broad, shallow bays. During the cooler months they drift out to deeper water and may travel some distance around the coast. They are bottom-feeders, dining mainly on small crustaceans, molluscs and tiny fish.

Hook, Line and Sinker

Rig are not a common recreational quarry, being most frequently taken in set nets during summer. They are best targeted by surfcasting into guts and channels along sandy beaches with a running rig and crabs for bait. They put up a dogged fight.

Food Qualities

A popular commercial species, rig is widely sold as lemon fish and is common in fish-and-chip shops. The flesh is firm, white and boneless but does not flake easily. It is suited to all cooking methods.

Piquant Grilled Rig

4–6 PORTIONS OF RIG
100 G BUTTER
2 TBSP LEMON JUICE
1 TSP LEMON ZEST
1 TSP PAPRIKA
WORCESTERSHIRE SAUCE
PARMESAN CHEESE
CHOPPED CHIVES
CRACKED PEPPER

• Heat the butter in a pan. Add the lemon juice, zest and paprika, a dash of Worcestershire sauce and a good sprinkle of Parmesan cheese. Mix well.
• Brush the fish pieces on both sides with the mixture and place on a greased baking tray. Grill for approximately 5 minutes per side.
• Sprinkle with chopped chives and cracked pepper before serving.

Bag limits

North 20
Combined finfish bag: 20
Minimum size: none
Minimum set-net mesh: 125 mm

Central/ Challenger 20
Combined finfish bag: 20
Minimum size: none
Minimum set-net mesh: 150 mm

South 5
Combined finfish bag: 30
Minimum size: none
Minimum set-net mesh: 150 mm

Red Cod

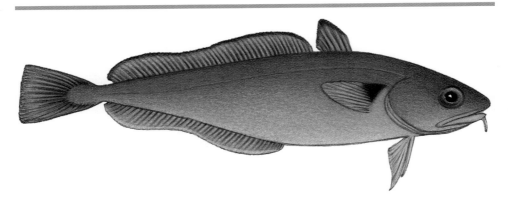

This slimy, catfishlike character is not commonly held in high regard except around Canterbury, where it is known as Akaroa cod. It is easily recognised by its small head and slender body, which tapers to a small, flat tail.

Its upper body is greyish red to reddish brown and its flanks are pinkish white.

There is a distinctive black blotch at the base of the small pectoral fin. The anal fin almost mirrors in shape and size the second — and longer — of two dorsal fins. A tiny barbel extends from the lower jaw. The scales are small, soft and easily dislodged. Average length is 40–70 cm, weight 1.5–2.5 kg.

Distribution

Red cod are found throughout New Zealand's coastal waters, from inshore out to 700 m. The biggest populations are around the South Island in 100–300 m. Schooling fish often found over sandy or muddy bottoms, red cod are voracious feeders, dining on a wide range of small bottom-living creatures. Larger specimens occasionally take quite big fish.

Hook, Line and Sinker

Red cod is frequently an undesirable by-catch, its rapacious feeding habits leading it to take any bait. It can be hooked on most common rigs. Canterbury surfcasters often target it over flat bottoms with ledger or running rigs with 5–6/0 hooks. It can also be taken in set nets.

rig	hook sizes											line weight							
	1/0	2/0	3/0	4/0	5/0	6/0	8/0	10/0	12/0	13/0	14/0	2	4	6	8	10	15	24	37
Stray line				●										●					
Ledger rig				●										●					
Running rig				●										●					
Flasher rig				●										●					

Live Bait	Trolling	Spinning	Jigs

Food Qualities

A very soft, moist flesh which flakes readily, it is low in fat and has a mild flavour. It needs to be chilled immediately to preserve its flavour and to make filleting easier. Suitable for most cooking methods, it is most commonly battered and deep-fried.

Red Cod in Tinfoil

4 RED COD FILLETS
CRACKED PEPPER
ZEST OF 1 LEMON
4 SPRING ONIONS, CHOPPED
2 TBSP CHOPPED BASIL
JUICE OF 2 LEMONS
OLIVE OIL

• Place each fillet in the centre of a sheet of foil. Liberally dust each fillet with cracked pepper, lemon zest, spring onions and basil.
• Squeeze the lemon juice over the fillets and drizzle with olive oil. Fold the foil over to make sealed parcels and bake for 10 minutes in an oven preheated to 200°C.

Bag limits

Northern/Central/ Challenger 20
Combined finfish bag: 20
Minimum size: 25 cm
Minimum set-net mesh: 100 mm

South 30
Combined finfish bag: 30
Minimum size: 25 cm
Minimum set-net mesh: 100 mm

Bastard Red Cod

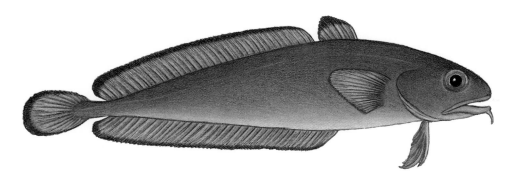

This little impostor is often mistaken for genuine red cod (see page 54), being similar in appearance, but it lacks the distinctive black pectoral blotch of its namesake.

It varies in colour from red to dark reddish brown and has an orange flush to the lips. The vertical fins are fringed with black.

The bastard red cod has a slender body similar in shape to that of the red cod. It averages 20–40 cm in length but can grow to around 60 cm.

Distribution

There is a northern bastard red cod, but the southern variety is more common. This is found mostly in southern waters to a depth of 250 m, although small numbers straggle north of East Cape. Unlike genuine red cod, bastard cod prefer rocky habitats, where they hide in holes and feed on a wide variety of small creatures.

Bag limits

All regions no limit
Minimum size: none
Minimum set-net mesh:
100 mm

Hook, Line and Sinker

Bastard red cod are usually a recreational by-catch, taken by anglers fishing for other species over reefs and heavy foul. Commonly caught on ledger rigs and 4–6/0 hooks or flasher rigs, they will take any bait.

Food Qualities

The flesh, like that of the red cod, is soft and moist and flakes easily. It has a bland flavour and is best baked with something to enhance the taste.

Red Moki

The red moki is a member of the morwong family, hence a relative of the tarakihi. It has a similarly deep, compressed, oval-shaped body extending to a broadish forked tail.

The eyes and head are small and the lips thick and fleshy. The body is pale reddish brown, with eight distinctive darker vertical bands down its length and through the fins.

The dorsal fin extends from the shoulder to the base of the tail, with spines along the front half. Red moki average 30–40 cm in length but can grow to around 60 cm. Slow-growing, they can live up to 60 years of age.

Distribution

The red moki prefers warmer waters, its range extending north from Cook Strait. It is a shallow-water fish, seldom venturing below 30 m, and is a resident of reefs and heavy foul, where its coloration provides good camouflage. Its diet consists mainly of small creatures filtered from sediment.

Hook, Line and Sinker

Red moki are generally taken in set nets over reefs, but are also a popular target for spear-fishers. The fact that they are resident all year and do not migrate makes them susceptible to overfishing.

Food Qualities

The flesh tends to be slightly dry but is tasty all the same. It is firm and suited to baking or poaching.

Bag limits

**North/Central/
Challenger 20**
Combined finfish bag: 20
Minimum size: 40 cm
Minimum set-net mesh:
115 mm

South 15
Combined finfish bag: 30
Minimum size: 40 cm
Minimum set-net mesh:
115 mm

Butterfly Perch

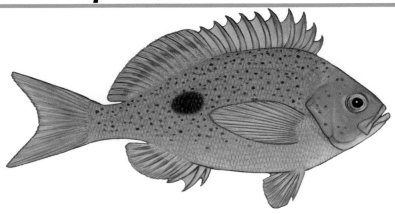

The butterfly perch is readily distinguished by a black blotch in the middle of each flank. It is reddish in colour along the back and pink on the flanks, with a slight blue flush all over. The lower flanks are often speckled with tiny black spots. The body is oval, deep and compressed.

The head is tiny in relation to the body, the mouth is small and the teeth are arranged in bands in both jaws.

The dorsal fin is long, and the pectoral fins are long and leaf-shaped. The anal fin has prominent spines along the front edge. Butterfly perch grow to around 35 cm in length.

Distribution

Butterfly perch are common in coastal waters around both the North and South Islands. They favour rocky areas down to around 50 m, and feed on small crabs, shrimps and small shellfish.

Hook, Line and Sinker

Usually taken as a by-catch, the butterfly perch puts up an erratic, fluttering fight when hooked. The small mouth dictates the use of light tackle and 1–2/0 hooks. Ledger rigs with tiny strip baits are effective, but success is most likely with flasher rigs or bait flies.

rig	hook sizes											line weight							
	1/0	2/0	3/0	4/0	5/0	6/0	8/0	10/0	12/0	13/0	14/0	2	4	6	8	10	15	24	37
Stray line																			
Ledger rig	●												●						
Running rig																			
Flasher rig	●												●						

Live Bait	Trolling	Spinning	Jigs

Food Qualities

Butterfly perch is often discarded but is in fact quite tasty. Fillets are small, firm and a little dry, so are best baked or lightly poached.

Seared Perch with Pan-fried Breadcrumbs

4 PORTIONS PERCH FILLETS
ROCK SALT
CRACKED PEPPER
OLIVE OIL
JUICE OF 1 LEMON

1 1/2 CUPS FRESH ROUGHLY
  CHOPPED BREADCRUMBS
HANDFUL CHOPPED FRESH MINT
1 TBSP CAPERS
ZEST OF A LEMON
CRACKED PEPPER

- Place perch fillets in a shallow dish and sprinkle with rock salt and a good belt of cracked pepper.
- Add a dash of olive oil to a pan and when hot, quickly sear the perch for about 60 seconds per side, turning once. Remove to a bowl, add a squeeze of lemon juice and place in the warmer.
- In the same pan add a dash more olive oil until a thin layer covers the bottom. Combine breadcrumbs, mint, capers, lemon zest and cracked pepper. Quickly fry the breadcrumb mix over a high heat until golden.
- Place fillets on serving plates, top with a sprinkle of the fried breadcrumbs and serve immediately with a fresh salad or steamed vegetables.

Bag limits

All regions no limit
Minimum size: none
Minimum set-net mesh:
100 mm

Sea Perch

This ugly little critter, commonly known as the scarpee, is an angel in disguise. It is distinguished by its big head, large eyes and wide mouth. It is brown and orange, with vertical bands along its length.

It has large pectoral fins and a broad tail, and the head and gill plates are covered with spines. Sea perch commonly grow to around 30 cm long but can reach 40 cm.

Distribution

The sea perch is most common south of East Cape. Reefs and foul ground down to around 50 m are its usual haunts. It is an aggressive predator, feeding on a variety of small fish.

Hook, Line and Sinker

While not commonly sought, sea perch are a doddle to catch over foul ground. They will take absolutely any bait and are most frequently caught on ledger rigs. They are suckers for lightly baited flasher rigs of any pattern, and will take small jigs played with a slow action, but they put up almost no fight. The mouth opens wide, giving the impression of a larger fish. Watch out for the spines — they deliver a painful, although nonpoisonous, sting.

rig	hook sizes											line weight							
	1/0	2/0	3/0	4/0	5/0	6/0	8/0	10/0	12/0	13/0	14/0	2	4	6	8	10	15	24	37
Stray line																			
Ledger rig					●												●		
Running rig																			
Flasher rig					●												●		

Live Bait	Trolling	Spinning	Jigs

Food Qualities

Sea perch make superb eating but can be fiddly to fillet. Large fish have a delicate white flesh suited to most cooking methods, but are probably best beheaded, scaled, gutted and deep-fried whole.

Crispy Oriental Sea Perch

Bag limits

All regions no limit
Minimum size: none
Minimum set-net mesh:
100 mm

4 WHOLE PERCH, BEHEADED,
  SCALED AND GUTTED
FLOUR
SALT
1 TBSP OLIVE OIL
1 CUP WATER
2 EGG WHITES
OIL FOR DEEP-FRYING

- In a large bowl, mix a cup of flour with a pinch of salt, then whisk in the oil and water to make a smooth batter.
- In a separate bowl whisk the egg whites until they peak, then fold them into the batter.

- Put a cup of flour and one of the fish into a plastic bag. Shake the bag to coat the fish liberally with flour. Repeat with the other fish.
- Dip each fish in the batter so it is well coated, then pop it into a wok of hot oil. Cook until crispy brown, turning once if the oil isn't deep enough to immerse the fish, then remove and drain on paper towels.
- Serve with the following lemon sauce:

Lemon Sauce

2 CUPS WATER
2 TSP CHICKEN STOCK POWDER
ZEST OF HALF A LEMON
1/2 CUP LEMON JUICE
1 TBSP BROWN SUGAR
1 TBSP CORNFLOUR

- Boil the water in a pan and dissolve the chicken stock powder. Bring to the boil again and add the zest, juice and sugar. Simmer for 2–3 minutes.
- Mix the cornflour with water to form a smooth paste. Stir this into the sauce until it boils and thickens.
- Spoon the sauce over the fish and serve.

Gurnard

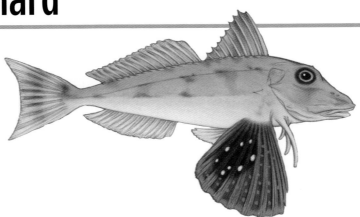

There is no mistaking this exotic-looking species. Its nickname, which is Carrot, clearly reflects its body shape and colour. It is reddish pink to brownish above and white below.

The rather bony head tapers to the front, imparting a shovel-like appearance, and the cylinder-shaped body tapers sharply from the shoulder to the tail. Huge colourful wing-shaped pectoral fins are another distinctive feature.

Average length is 30–50 cm, with large specimens reaching 60 cm. Gurnard are fairly fast-growing, reaching maturity around the age of two, but seldom live past ten.

Distribution

Gurnard are widespread throughout New Zealand waters over open, sandy bottoms down to around 150 m. They feed mainly on small crabs and shrimps, and sometimes small fish. Gurnard are very common in shallow bays and coastal regions, which makes them a prime target species.

Hook, Line and Sinker

Gurnard are not renowned for their turn of speed, stalking their prey cautiously as they sift along the bottom. They are best targeted by drifting ledger or flasher rigs with small baits along the bottom, particularly the sandy faces that slope into channels. Fishing from sandy beaches into channels and guts is another common method. Gurnard will take a variety of baits, particularly fresh shellfish, as well as small jigs cast out and skittered erratically across the bottom. Many anglers don't rate them as great sport, but on light tackle — 4–6 kg — they put up an aggressive fight.

rig	hook sizes											line weight							
	1/0	2/0	3/0	4/0	5/0	6/0	8/0	10/0	12/0	13/0	14/0	2	4	6	8	10	15	24	37
Stray line					●	●								●					
Ledger rig					●	●								●					
Running rig					●	●								●					
Flasher rig					●	●								●					

Live Bait	Trolling	Spinning	Jigs

Food Qualities

The flesh is firm and low in fat and has a pinkish tinge. It cooks white and has a delicate flavour. Suited to all cooking methods, it is best lightly fried or grilled.

Grilled Lemon Gurnard

4–6 GURNARD FILLETS
50 G BUTTER
1 TBSP CHOPPED FRESH BASIL
2 TBSP LEMON JUICE
GRATED ZEST OF A LEMON
CRACKED PEPPER TO TASTE

• Soften the butter and blend in the basil, juice, zest and cracked pepper.
• Baste the top of each fillet with a liberal quantity of the mixture and grill for 5 minutes or until just cooked.

Bag limits

North 20
Combined finfish bag: 20
Minimum size: none
Minimum set-net mesh: 100 mm

Central 20
Combined finfish bag: 20
Minimum size: none
Minimum set-net mesh: 100 mm

Challenger 20
Combined finfish bag: 20
Minimum size: none
Minimum set-net mesh: 100 mm

South 30
Combined finfish bag: 30
Minimum size: none
Minimum set-net mesh: 100 mm

Pink Maomao

The pink maomao is unrelated to the blue maomao, being of the sea perch rather than the drummer family. It has a narrow, elongated body and a broad, slightly forked tail.

It is bright pink and occasionally has a smattering of yellow markings. The head and pectoral fins tend towards orange, and the dorsal fin is prominent. Pink maomao average 30–40 cm in length but can grow to around 50 cm.

Distribution

Pink maomao are most common in warmer, northern waters but extend as far south as Cook Strait. They are often found around offshore islands, reefs and exposed headlands, from shallows down to about 200 m. They are schooling fish that feed on plankton and small shrimps.

Hook, Line and Sinker

Pink maomao isn't really a target species and is most likely to be taken as a by-catch. It can be caught on a small hook lightly baited with shellfish and drifted in the current, or on a small flasher rig that resembles a shrimp pattern.

Bag limits

All regions no limit
Minimum size: none
Minimum set-net mesh:
100 mm

Food Qualities

The flesh is firm, white and of good quality. It is suited to frying, grilling, baking and marinating.

Elephant Fish

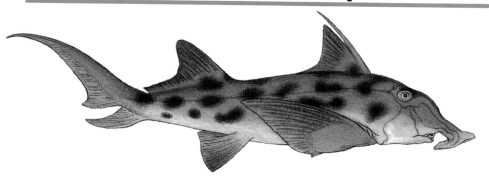

The elephant fish is a shark relative but distinguished by its smooth skin. It has a silver-grey upper body, covered with brownish blotches, and a silver-white belly.

Its sharklike appearance and fleshy, trunklike snout make it easy to identify.

Elephant fish average 60–90 cm in length but can grow to 120 cm and weigh as much as 4 kg. They are fast-growing but have a short lifespan.

Distribution

Elephant fish are most common along the east coast of the South Island, down to 200 m, but extend north in limited numbers to Cape Egmont and Hawke's Bay. They favour shallower regions, especially in spring, when females migrate inshore to lay their egg capsules. Elephant fish feed on small crustaceans, molluscs and other tiny creatures that inhabit sediment.

Hook, Line and Sinker

Elephant fish are most commonly taken by set-netting shallow bays during the spawning season, but may also be caught on a running rig with small hooks and shellfish bait. They are good fighting fish on light tackle.

Food Qualities

The flesh is firm and white. It is suited to all cooking methods and makes excellent eating.

Bag limits

⚠ **North/Central/ Challenger 20**
Combined finfish bag: 20
Minimum size: none
Minimum set-net mesh:
150 mm

✅ **South 5**
Combined finfish bag: 30
Minimum size: none
Minimum set-net mesh:
150 mm

Goatfish

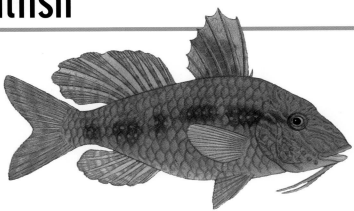

This exotic-looking fish is most easily identified by its two long barbels, which extend beneath the lower jaw. The body is elongated, compressed and covered with large scales.

There are two dorsal fins, the second similar in shape to the anal fin but slightly larger.

Coloration is pink to reddish, with blue stripes on the head and rows of blue spots the length of the body. The flanks are also patterned with mauve and yellow. The mouth and teeth are small. Goatfish average 10–20 cm in length but grow to around 30 cm.

Distribution

An inhabitant of warmer coastal waters, the goatfish is heavily distributed around the North Island, although its range extends to the top of the South Island. Its preferred habitat is reefs and foul down to 50 m. It feeds on shrimps, small crabs and other marine invertebrates, using its barbels to detect them as it sifts through sand and mud around the reef perimeter.

Hook, Line and Sinker

Bag limits

All regions no limit
Minimum size: none
Minimum set-net mesh:
100 mm

Goatfish are usually taken as by-catch, and put up a pathetic struggle compared with popular target species. Light gear with 1–3/0 hooks and tiny bait is best. Flasher rigs that resemble shrimp patterns are effective. Goatfish can also be taken by drift-fishing over reefs, or with the aid of berley along a reef fringe, but are most commonly caught in set nets or by spear-fishers.

Food Qualities

An underrated species, goatfish are superb eating. The firm, distinctively flavoured flesh is ideal marinated, baked or fried.

Blue Mackerel

The blue mackerel — also often called English mackerel — is related to the tuna family, not the jack mackerels. The back is a distinctive metallic blue-green colour and patterned with darker, wavy lines that fade to a series of lighter spots along the sides and then silver-white on the underside.

Blue mackerel are tunalike in shape, being quite rounded, with a small, conical head and large eyes. They are commonly 30–45 cm long but may grow to 55 cm.

Distribution

Blue mackerel are widespread around the North Island and the top of the South Island, where they school, feeding on krill, larvae, fish eggs and small fish. They are common in the coastal belt, but strong migrational patterns mean numbers can vary.

Hook, Line and Sinker

Blue mackerel are not commonly targeted by recreational fishers — they are usually caught in set nets — but they provide excellent sport on light tackle, taking small trolled lures, jigs and flasher rigs.

Food Qualities

The flesh is dark, flaky and high in oil. It is excellent smoked, canned or marinated.

Bag limits

All regions no limit

Minimum size: none

Minimum set-net mesh:
100 mm

Yellow-eyed Mullet

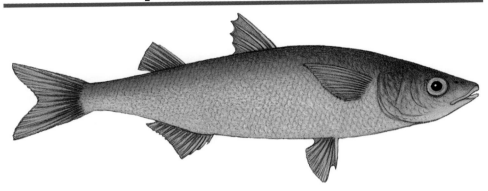

This is a slender fish with a pointed head and a distinctive yellow eye. It is blue-green to slightly olive above and silvery white below. There are two dorsal fins, and the scales are delicate and dislodge freely during handling. The yellow-eyed mullet is fast-growing, reaching some 40 cm in length, and lives for about seven years.

Distribution

Yellow-eyed mullet are widespread throughout New Zealand's inshore coastal waters, bays, harbours and estuaries. They will often travel some distance up rivers with the tide in search of food. They feed primarily on algae and other tiny organisms. Spawning takes place in summer and autumn.

Hook, Line and Sinker

Yellow-eyed mullet are an important recreational catch for budding young anglers, especially around wharves, where they are commonly taken on tiny Sabiki and ledger rigs with morsels of cut bait or in small bait traps. They are also caught with set bait nets in shallow bays, estuaries and harbours, and with dragnets in river mouths.

Bag limits

All regions no limit
Minimum size: none
Minimum set-net mesh:
25 mm

Food Qualities

Yellow-eyed mullet is not considered prime eating and is more likely to end up as bait. The flesh has a darkish tinge and a delicate texture. It is used predominantly for rollmops but is excellent smoked.

Koheru

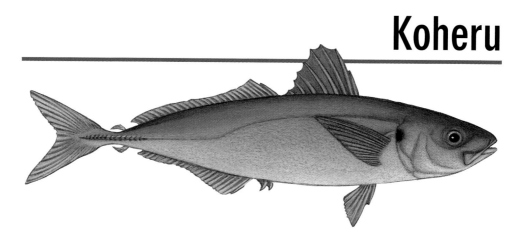

The koheru has a slender, rounded body covered in small scales. It is a brilliant bluish green above and silvery white below, the sides often have a golden flush, and a dark blotch is visible on the upper gill plate.

It has a high, spiny dorsal fin, and the body tapers to a sharply forked tail. Koheru are schooling fish and grow to between 25 and 40 cm.

Distribution

Koheru are coastal fish, found above East Cape but more common further north. They feed on small crabs, shrimps and other crustaceans and occasionally take small fish or larvae.

Hook, Line and Sinker

Commonly sought as live bait, koheru are attracted by berley and most effectively targeted with light tackle, small flasher rigs and ledger rigs with tiny hooks and baits. They can be taken at night under wharf lights.

Food Qualities

Koheru is not generally eaten but is fine marinated.

Bag limits

All regions no limit
Minimum size: none
Minimum set-net mesh:
100 mm

Jack Mackerel

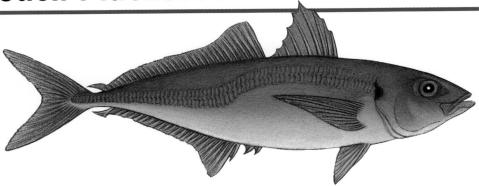

The jack mackerel — also known as horse mackerel — is greenish above, with an almost metallic sheen and faint brownish bands, and has a white belly.

The body is streamlined and has prominent ridged scales along the lateral line, which are more pronounced towards the forked tail. The head is slender and the mouth angled slightly up, with a slightly projecting lower jaw.

Jack mackerel average 30–40 cm in length but grow to 50 cm. They are fast-growing and live for 15–25 years.

Distribution

Jack mackerel are pelagic, although they will spend time near the bottom, especially when attracted by berley. They are widespread throughout New Zealand waters down to 300 m. They feed predominantly on zooplankton but also take small fish and larvae.

Hook, Line and Sinker

Jack mackerel are generally targeted for live bait and provide great fun when taken on ultralight tackle with Sabiki rigs, small baited flasher rigs or ledger rigs with small hooks. They adopt an aggressive darting motion when hooked. They are often caught in bait set nets.

Food Qualities

The flesh is dark but lightens when cooked, and it has a medium fat content. It is popular smoked, but is also good baked or made into pies and casseroles. It has a mild-to-strong flavour, depending on fat content.

Smoked Mackerel Chowder

500 G SMOKED JACK MACKEREL, BONED AND FLAKED
500 ML MILK
2 TBSP OLIVE OIL
2 LARGE POTATOES, PEELED AND DICED
1 LARGE ONION, PEELED AND CHOPPED
100 ML DRY WHITE WINE
500 ML CHICKEN STOCK
SALT
CRACKED PEPPER

• In a saucepan, bring the milk just to the boil. Remove from the heat and add the fish. Leave to stand for 5–10 minutes. Drain the milk and keep to one side.
• Heat the oil in a pan and sauté the potatoes and onions for about 10 minutes. Add the wine and cook until the liquid has reduced by half. Add the stock and milk.
• Simmer until the potatoes are tender. Whizz the mixture in a food processor until smooth.
• Return to the pan, gradually stir in the fish and season with salt and cracked pepper. Reheat gently and serve with croutons or hot toast.

Bag limits

All regions no limit
Minimum size: none
Minimum set-net mesh: 100 mm

Pilchard

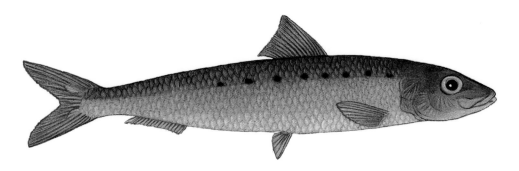

The pilchard has a long, slender, rounded body that is dark blue along the back, greenish on the sides and silver below. A row of black spots extends along either flank. The dorsal fin is small and the tail small and forked. Pilchards average around 15–20 cm in length but can grow up to 25 cm.

Distribution

Common in warmer inshore waters, pilchards are most abundant from the Marlborough Sounds and Tasman Bay to Northland. They are surface-schooling and feed on plankton, and are often found together with sprats and anchovies.

Hook, Line and Sinker

Pilchards are largely a commercial catch, but when they are schooling on the surface they can be taken by recreational fishers with scoop nets.

Food Qualities

Pilchards are predominantly a bait species, but they have a soft, oily flesh suitable for canning, pickling and smoking.

Bag limits

All regions no limit

Minimum size: none

Minimum set-net mesh:

25 mm

Piper

The piper — also known as garfish — is easy to distinguish because it looks like a miniature, skinny marlin. The body is long and slender, greenish blue above, silver along the flanks and white underneath.

The back is usually covered with brown flecks. The lower jaw extends like a beak and is tipped with orange.

The piper's dorsal and anal fins are well to the rear of the body, and the lower lobe of the tail is larger than the upper. Piper average 20–25 cm in length but can grow to around 40 cm. They are fast-growing and can live for up to six years.

Distribution

Piper are widely distributed throughout New Zealand's inshore waters and are common in shallow bays and estuaries, where they school on the surface. They feed on algae, grasses and tiny animals and larvae.

Hook, Line and Sinker

Piper can be caught in a variety of ways, the most common of which is to drag a fine-mesh net through a gutter or over a bed of sea grass. They are attracted by lights at night-time and can be taken with a scoop net in shallow areas. On ultralight tackle they can be caught with tiny baited hooks — fresh shellfish is best — suspended under a float, or with small bait flies.

Bag limits

All regions no limit
Minimum size: none
Minimum set-net mesh:
25 mm

Food Qualities

Piper have a delicate, almost translucent flesh that is not dissimilar to whitebait in flavour. They are best lightly fried and the bones will peel away easily with the backbone once cooked.

Barracouta

The barracouta is a member of the snake mackerel family and the bane of fishermen. A vicious predator renowned for hunting in packs, it has razor-sharp teeth, designed for tearing, which make short work of traces and terminal tackle.

It is easily identified by its long, slender, laterally flattened body, iridescent silver-chrome sheen and bluish back.

The barracouta has a snakelike head, large eyes and a long, spiny dorsal sail. A second, smaller dorsal fin rises behind the first. The body tapers to a pronounced forked tail. Barracouta are fast-growing and can live for up to 10 years.

Distribution

Barracouta are widespread around New Zealand but most prolific from Cook Strait south. They occupy a broad habitat, ranging throughout the water column from inshore estuaries to depths of more than 200 metres over the continental shelf. They feed mainly on small fish.

Hook, Line and Sinker

Barracouta are generally not targeted by fishers, being frequently infested with worm, but are a common by-catch. They will attack anything flashy and can easily destroy nylon rigs, so are best targeted with a wire trace and large hooks rigged with large strip baits. They will take shiny jigs and provide excellent sport on light tackle, the fight being characterised by long, powerful, scything runs.

rig	hook sizes											line weight							
	1/0	2/0	3/0	4/0	5/0	6/0	8/0	10/0	12/0	13/0	14/0	2	4	6	8	10	15	24	37
Stray line					●										●				
Ledger rig					●										●				
Running rig					●										●				
Flasher rig					●										●				

Live Bait	Trolling	Spinning	Jigs

Food Qualities

Not usually considered suitable for eating because many are worm-infested, barracouta has a delicate flavour and a medium fat content. The dark flesh is best suited to quick frying or smoking.

Smoked Barracouta with Avocado Dressing

4 PORTIONS OF SMOKED
  BARRACOUTA
1 PACKET FRESH PASTA
SALT
1 TBSP OLIVE OIL
1 RIPE AVOCADO
1 CUP SOUR CREAM
1/4 CUP OLIVE OIL
6 DROPS TABASCO SAUCE
CRACKED PEPPER

- Place pasta in water brought to the boil with a dash of salt and 1 tbsp olive oil. Cook pasta until *al dente* and drain.
- In a shallow pan lightly poach barracouta until warmed through. Drain and remove to a warmer.
- In a blender combine avocado, sour cream, olive oil, Tabasco and cracked pepper to taste until smooth.
- Arrange a helping of pasta in the centre of each plate, place a portion of fish on top and drizzle over a good measure of the avocado dressing. Serve with a crisp side salad and fresh bread.

Bag limits

South 30
Combined finfish bag: 30
Minimum size: none
Minimum set-net mesh:
100 mm

Other regions
no limit
Minimum size: none
Minimum set-net mesh:
100 mm

Grey Mullet

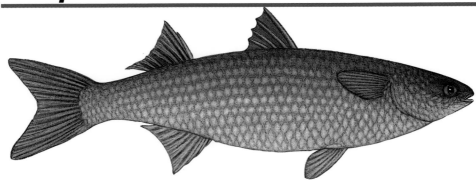

The grey mullet is distinguished from the yellow-eyed by its broad, flat head and snout. It is dark silvery grey above, with a greenish tinge and faint stripes, and silvery below. It has large, firm scales compared with the yellow-eyed, and two dorsal fins.

Grey mullet are commonly around 40 cm in length but can reach 60 cm and weigh 5 kg. They are fast-growing, with a lifespan of up to 10 years.

Distribution

Grey mullet favour warmer northern waters but extend as far south as Tasman Bay, although they are now rare in this area. They prefer the sheltered waters of harbours, bays and estuaries. They feed predominantly on algae and other organic matter on the seafloor but may also eat tiny marine animals.

Bag limits

⬆ **North 30**
(separate from combined
finfish bag limits)
Minimum size: none
Minimum set-net mesh:
90 mm

➤ **Central/
Challenger 20**
Combined finfish bag: 20
Minimum size: none
Minimum set-net mesh:
100 mm

▼ **South 30**
Combined finfish bag: 30
Minimum size: none
Minimum set-net mesh:
100 mm

Hook, Line and Sinker

Grey mullet are most commonly caught in set nets or by beach seines but will occasionally take a tiny baited hook.

Food Qualities

The flesh has a darkish tinge. Its high fat content makes it suitable for smoking, but it can have a strong flavour when cooked using other methods.

Sprat

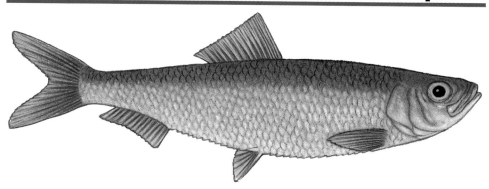

Sometimes referred to as the New Zealand herring or sardine, the sprat comes in two species — the slender and the stout. It is similar in shape to the pilchard, but tends to be shorter and deeper about the middle, with a thin body. It has a small pointed head, a small mouth, large eyes and a forked tail. Dark blue above and silvery along the sides and belly, the sprat may also have a greenish tinge. A distinct row of sharp scales runs under the belly. Sprats average 8–10 cm in length but can grow to around 15 cm.

Distribution

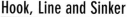

Sprats are most common in South Island waters, but are scattered around the coast as far north as Auckland. Both pelagic and inshore fish, they prefer the bottom and midwater zones in the cooler seasons and shoal near the surface in summer. During winter, sprats move inshore to spawn and are a common sight in estuaries, bays and harbours.

Hook, Line and Sinker

Most young anglers get started with sprats and other small species. Sprats can be taken on light tackle using ledger rigs and tiny baited hooks. A Sabiki bait fly with a morsel of bait is both entertaining and productive. Small bait traps are useful, while rice, breadcrumbs or berley tossed into the water will attract sprats.

Bag limits

All regions no limit
Minimum size: none

Food Qualities

Not considered an eating species, they can, however, be canned or smoked, although they are more important as a source of fresh bait. The flesh is dark and oily.

Hapuku

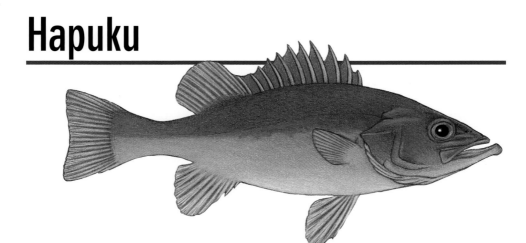

Otherwise known as groper, the hapuku is the most commonly targeted deep-water species in New Zealand. It is similar in appearance to the bass but has a more slender, elongated body and is easily distinguished by its protruding lower jaw.

Also distinctive are its counter-shaded body markings — blue-grey to grey-brown on top, grey to white beneath.

Slow-growing, hapuku can reach around 2 m in length and exceed 50 kg in weight, although catches of 10–30 kg are more common. Hapuku in excess of 100 kg have been reported.

Distribution

Hapuku are found throughout New Zealand waters, including around the Chatham Islands, over foul ground from 30 to 400 m. However, while once common along shallow inshore reefs, they have become largely limited in their range by fishing pressure to deeper offshore reefs of around 100–300 m, although juveniles will swim into shallow water and over flat bottoms in summer and can be caught in as little as 10 m.

Hapuku are migratory and spawn in winter. They are scavengers and feed on a wide variety of food, such as squid, fish and crayfish.

Hook, Line and Sinker

The most common method of catching hapuku is drifting large cut baits on a 2–3-hook ledger rig over reefs. Large circle hooks (12–16/0) are required, with the bait hooked once near one end. Hapuku will take live baits and can be caught with large flashy jigs in shallower waters.

rig	hook sizes											line weight							
	1/0	2/0	3/0	4/0	5/0	6/0	8/0	10/0	12/0	13/0	14/0	2	4	6	8	10	15	24	37
Stray line																			
Ledger rig								●										●	
Running rig																			
Flasher rig						●												●	

Live Bait	Trolling	Spinning	Jigs

Food Qualities

The flesh is white, firm and succulent. Prepared either as fillets or, from smaller fish, as steaks, it is suited to all types of cooking but is best baked over a moderate heat.

Hapuku Steaks with Lemon Sauce

4 HAPUKU STEAKS
1 CUP LIQUID CHICKEN STOCK
JUICE OF A LEMON
ZEST OF HALF A LEMON
1 TBSP CHOPPED CAPERS
50 G BUTTER
50 G FLOUR

• Fry the steaks in a hot pan for 3–4 minutes either side or until medium-cooked. Remove to a warming drawer.
• In the same pan, heat the chicken stock to a simmer. Add the juice, zest and capers.
• Blend the butter and flour and gradually stir into the stock mixture so it thickens. Pour the sauce over the steaks and serve.

Bag limits

All regions 5

Combined bag: 5 hapuku, bass and kingfish, with no more than 3 kingfish

Minimum set-net mesh: 160 mm

Bluenose

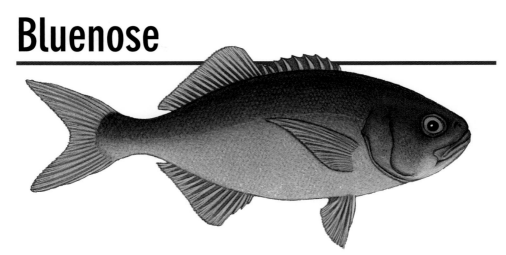

The bluenose is a member of the warehou family. It is distinguished by its large mouth, large eyes, blunt head and long, oval-shaped body. Its back is a dark bluish grey, blending to metallic grey and silver along the flanks. It usually weighs 10–15 kg but can tip the scales at as much as 30 kg.

Distribution

The bluenose is found over foul ground all round the New Zealand coast at depths of 100–500 m. It is most commonly taken in Cook Strait and the Bay of Plenty. A schooling fish that enjoys a varied diet of squid, crustaceans, small fish and jellyfish, it feeds from the bottom through to the middle of the water column.

Hook, Line and Sinker

Bluenose inhabit the same areas as hapuku and bass, so are not targeted specifically but form part of a wider catch. They can be seen on a sounder, schooling just off the bottom, often above hapuku and bass. They are taken by drift-fishing over reefs with large cut baits or whole fish attached to heavy ledger rigs with recurve hooks. The bluenose is a strong fish that will fight all the way to the surface.

rig	hook sizes											line weight							
	1/0	2/0	3/0	4/0	5/0	6/0	8/0	10/0	12/0	13/0	14/0	2	4	6	8	10	15	24	37
Stray line																			
Ledger rig								●										●	
Running rig																			
Flasher rig						●												●	

Live Bait	Trolling	Spinning	Jigs

Food Qualities

Bluenose is a very popular eating fish. It has a forgiving flesh that is hard to ruin in the kitchen. Its thick succulent fillets suit all cooking methods.

Oven-bag Bluenose

4 MEDIUM-SIZED BLUENOSE
  FILLETS
2 TSP CRUSHED GARLIC
2 TSP CRUSHED GINGER
1 TBSP MILD MUSTARD
1 TBSP LIGHT SOY SAUCE
1 TBSP SWEET CHILLI SAUCE
2 TBSP OLIVE OIL
2 TBSP CHOPPED FRESH BASIL
1 CUP HALVED SMALL BUTTON
  MUSHROOMS
RIND OF A LEMON CUT INTO
  STRIPS
JUICE OF A LEMON

- Arrange the fillets flat in an oven bag. Mix the other ingredients in a bowl and pour them over the fish.
- Seal the bag and bake at 200°C for 15–20 minutes or until just cooked. Leave to stand for 5 minutes before serving.

Bag limits

🔺 **North 20**
Combined finfish bag: 20
Minimum size: none
Minimum set-net mesh: 160 mm

▶ **Central 20**
Combined finfish bag: 20
Minimum size: none
Minimum set-net mesh: 160 mm

Challenger 20
Combined finfish bag: 20
Minimum size: none
Minimum set-net mesh: 160 mm

🔻 **South 30**
Combined finfish bag: 30
Minimum size: none
Minimum set-net mesh: 160 mm

Blue Warehou

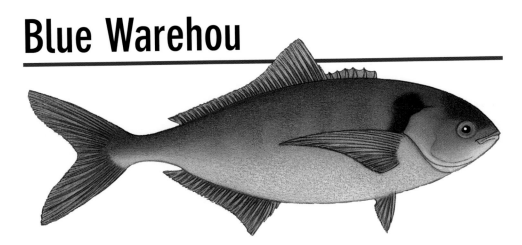

The blue warehou — also called the common warehou — is bluish green along the back and upper body but with a darker head and a black patch by the pectoral fin.

It has an iridescent sheen that fades to silvery white about the belly. The body is slender, flat and oval-shaped, and the pectoral fin is long and tapering.

Average length is 40–60 cm and weight about 4 kg, but large fish may be as long as 80 cm. Blue warehou are moderately fast-growing and live to around 10 years old.

Distribution

Blue warehou prefer cooler water so are most common in Cook Strait and around the South Island. Small populations are found in North Island waters but mostly south of the Bay of Plenty. They range from coastal shallows to a depth of 250 m over the mid-continental shelf, schooling in open water or around reefs, even in shallow bays. Spawning occurs during spring in deeper water.

Hook, Line and Sinker

Blue warehou feed on small planktonic creatures so are best targeted with pink flasher rigs resembling krill. They congregate in huge schools down to 200 m and are taken in the midwater column above reefs or over open areas. They take small jigs, and juveniles can be caught in set nets close to shore.

rig	hook sizes											line weight							
	1/0	2/0	3/0	4/0	5/0	6/0	8/0	10/0	12/0	13/0	14/0	2	4	6	8	10	15	24	37
Stray line																			
Ledger rig																			
Running rig																			
Flasher rig	●														●				

Live Bait	Trolling	Spinning	Jigs

Food Qualities

The flesh is firm and pinkish with a medium fat content. It is suited to light frying or baking. Warehou also make excellent sashimi and are nice marinated and superb when smoked.

Marinated Blue Warehou

500 G WAREHOU FILLETS
JUICE OF 2 LARGE LEMONS OR LIMES
1 ONION
1 GREEN PEPPER
2 CLOVES GARLIC
1 FRESH CHILLI, SEEDED
1 TOMATO
300 ML CREAM OR COCONUT MILK

• Cut the fillets into bite-sized cubes and marinate in the juice at room temperature for 1–2 hours, turning occasionally. Drain excess juice.
• Dice the onion, green pepper, garlic, chilli and tomato and combine with the fish. Pour the cream or coconut milk over the top and leave to stand for half an hour to allow the flavours to mingle.

Bag limits

⚫ **South 15**
Combined finfish bag: 30
Minimum size: none
Minimum set-net mesh: 100 mm

Other regions no limit
Minimum size: none
Minimum set-net mesh: 100 mm

Bass

Bass is a large deep-water species, similar to hapuku but distinguished by its rounder head and non-protruding lower jaw. It is bluish grey or greyish brown in colour and has a short, spiky dorsal fin and a stout body. A slow-growing species, bass can reach some 2 m in length and weigh over 100 kg.

Distribution

Bass are common throughout New Zealand's deeper coastal waters, where they frequent reefs to depths of over 300 m. They are especially abundant in Cook Strait and from the Bay of Islands north to the Three Kings Islands. While bass can be taken on reefs at 100 m or less, fishing pressure has limited the best catches to much deeper water.

Hook, Line and Sinker

Bass inhabit the same territory as hapuku but range deeper. The most effective method of targeting them is drift-fishing over deep reefs and pinnacles with 24–37 kg tackle, heavily weighted ledger rigs with two or three droppers armed with 14–16/0 circle hooks and whole dead baits or large cut baits. Whole baits need be hooked once only, through the head or tail, as this allows them to move in the current. Bites at such depths as bass inhabit are most easily detected with nonstretch superbraid lines. Over shallow reefs bass will take a large jig presented in a slow yo-yo manner.

rig	hook sizes											line weight							
	1/0	2/0	3/0	4/0	5/0	6/0	8/0	10/0	12/0	13/0	14/0	2	4	6	8	10	15	24	37
Stray line																			
Ledger rig										●							●		
Running rig																			
Flasher rig										●							●		

Live Bait	Trolling	Spinning	Jigs

Food Qualities

Considered a premium table fish, bass is suited to all cooking techniques, although its thick fillets are most conveniently baked. Fillets can be taken from the upper or the lower body, the belly flaps being considered the sweetest. Cut with the grain to make manageable portions for frying and grilling.

Baked Bass

500–800 G BASS FILLETS
CRACKED PEPPER
2 TBSP CHILLI SAUCE
2 TOMATOES, FINELY DICED
1 SPRING ONION, CHOPPED
2 TBSP LEMON JUICE
1 CUP SOUR CREAM
PARMESAN CHEESE
1 TBSP CHOPPED CHIVES

• Layer the fillets in a greased oven dish and season with cracked pepper. Mix the chilli sauce, tomatoes, spring onion and lemon juice with the sour cream and pour over the fish. Dust with Parmesan cheese.
• Cover the fish and bake at 180°C for 30 minutes. Remove from the oven and stand uncovered for 5 minutes. Sprinkle with the chives and more Parmesan.

Bag limits

All regions 5
Combined finfish bag:
5 hapuku, bass and kingfish, with no more than 3 kingfish
Minimum size: none
Minimum set-net mesh: 160 mm

Trumpeter

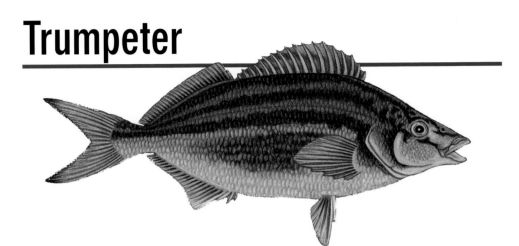

The trumpeter is considered a splendid fighting fish. Its body has an elongated oval shape and can be quite deep in older fish. The back is olive green, the belly yellowish.

Three horizontal stripes of yellow and light brown run the length of the body, making for easy identification. Trumpeter can grow to around a metre in length and up to 20 kg in weight, but are most common at half this size.

Distribution

Trumpeter are reef-dwellers, bigger fish preferring deeper reefs further offshore than smaller fish. They are most abundant south of Cook Strait, with good populations around the South Island's southern coast and Stewart Island. Pockets are found in North Island waters, particularly around Hawke's Bay and East Cape. The deeper reefs of the Bay of Plenty appear to mark the northern extremity of their range.

After spawning over deep reefs in winter, trumpeter migrate to shallower waters for the summer. Larger adult fish seem to be territorial, which could indicate a susceptibility to heavy fishing pressure.

Hook, Line and Sinker

Trumpeter inhabit the same places as hapuku, bass and bluenose and can be taken on the same rig. Usually a two-hook ledger rig with fresh bait or a small live bait drifted close to the bottom will prove successful. In shallower waters, down to 50 m, a medium-sized jig bounced above the bottom is effective, while baited flasher rigs are good for smaller fish. Trumpeter are schooling fish, so when located can provide excellent sport.

rig	hook sizes											line weight							
	1/0	2/0	3/0	4/0	5/0	6/0	8/0	10/0	12/0	13/0	14/0	2	4	6	8	10	15	24	37
Stray line																			
Ledger rig					●												●		
Running rig				●													●		
Flasher rig				●													●		

Live Bait	Trolling	Spinning	Jigs

Food Qualities

Trumpeter benefit from careful handling and are best killed, filleted and chilled immediately after being caught. The flesh has a fine texture and medium-strong flavour and is suited to all cooking methods.

Mediterranean Fish Bake

500–800 G TRUMPETER FILLETS
1–2 LARGE TOMATOES, DICED
2 TBSP CHOPPED BASIL
GRATED ZEST OF HALF A LEMON
JUICE OF A LEMON
1 TBSP OLIVE OIL
1 TBSP SESAME SEEDS
2 SPRING ONIONS, CHOPPED
1/4 TSP SALT
A GOOD DOSE OF CRACKED
  PEPPER

• Place the fillets flat in an oven bag.
• Put all the other ingredients in a bowl and mix thoroughly. Spoon the mixture into the oven bag, then seal the bag and toss it until the fillets are well coated. Leave it to stand for 30 minutes.
• Bake for 20–30 minutes in an oven preheated to 200°C. Serve with mashed potatoes and fresh vegetables.

Bag limits

 South 15
Combined finfish bag: 30
Minimum size: none
Minimum set-net mesh:
100 mm

Other regions no limit
Minimum size: none
Minimum set-net mesh:
100 mm

Ling

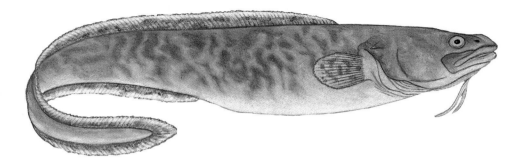

The ling is an ugly, slimy devil that belongs to a group of fishes called cusk eels. It has a long, round body that tapers to a long, flat tail. It is easily recognised by its varied colouring — reddish pink above, a golden hue on the sides, and mottled brown markings along both the back and flanks.

The scales are very fine and usually covered in heavy slime.

The ling has a large mouth with numerous small, sharp teeth. It is slow-growing and averages around 100 cm in length but can grow to 160 cm and weigh around 20 kg.

Distribution

Ling are common throughout New Zealand waters but most prolific south of Cook Strait. Their range extends from deep coastal reefs down to around 700 m. They can also be found over flat bottoms, and small ones will occasionally enter harbours and shallow bays. They are voracious predators, preying on a wide variety of fish, squid and crabs.

Bag limits

South 30

Combined finfish bag: 30

Minimum size: none

Other regions
no limit

Minimum size: none

Hook, Line and Sinker

Usually a deep-water by-catch, ling are most readily taken over deep reefs and ledges on a heavily weighted ledger rig with large recurve hooks and baits. They are not spectacular fighters, being more inclined to put up a dogged struggle. Gear of 24 kg is standard, with 100 kg trace and hooks in the 12–14/0 range.

Food Qualities

Difficult to fillet, ling is course and can be quite dry. The flesh is best cut into thin slivers before cooking. Poaching, baking or smoking are recommended techniques.

Red Snapper

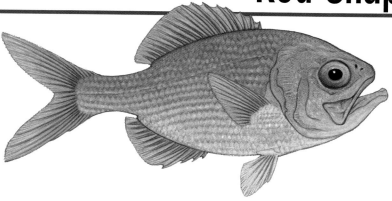

The red snapper is deep-bodied, with large eyes, spiny gill plates and an upturned mouth. It is golden-orange to red all over, with darkish red bands along the body.

The scales are rough with sharp edges, and the fins have prominent spines, making the fish hard to handle.

Red snapper average 30–40 cm in length but may reach 60 cm and weigh 5 kg.

Distribution

Red snapper are found in New Zealand coastal waters — most commonly in the north — from 20 to 400 m, their favoured habitat being large reefs and overhangs. They are believed to be largely nocturnal and to feed at night on plankton in the middle of the water column.

Hook, Line and Sinker

Red snapper are usually a by-catch of attempts to hook deep-water bottom-dwellers. They can be taken on a lightly baited ledger rig or on a flasher rig with recurve hooks of around 6/0. While depth and terrain usually dictate heavy tackle, red snapper put up a lively fight on lighter gear. Braid is definitely an advantage. Try fishing towards dusk along the face of a drop-off into deep water.

Bag limits

All regions no limit
Minimum size: none

Food Qualities

The flesh is white and moist and has a delicate texture and flavour and a medium fat content. Suited to all cooking methods, it is best lightly grilled or smoked.

King Tarakihi

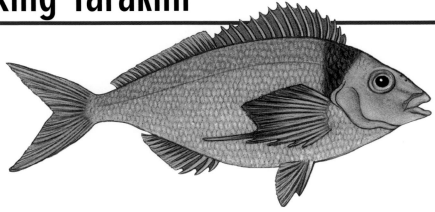

This species has only recently been identified but has rapidly become a popular target for recreational anglers. It is similar in appearance to the common tarakihi (see page 18) but grows much larger — to over 60 cm and around 7 kg.

It is distinguished from its cousin by black tips on its pectoral fins, its lighter black shoulder marking and a slight purple tinge to the upper body.

Distribution

The king tarakihi is not as widespread as the common, preferring warmer, northern waters. It is abundant over reef structures around the Three Kings Islands and is found in pockets about the Bay of Plenty and East Cape. Isolated catches have been reported along the southeast coast of the North Island. It is commonly caught around foul ground from about 50 m down.

Hook, Line and Sinker

Frequently a deep-water by-catch, the king tarakihi puts up a spectacular scrap on lighter tackle. It is generally taken on ledger rigs drifted over reefs and can take a much larger hook than the common tarakihi. Baited flasher rigs are very effective with a variety of small strip baits.

rig	hook sizes											line weight							
	1/0	2/0	3/0	4/0	5/0	6/0	8/0	10/0	12/0	13/0	14/0	2	4	6	8	10	15	24	37
Stray line																			
Ledger rig					●													●	
Running rig																			
Flasher rig					●													●	

Live Bait	Trolling	Spinning	Jigs

Food Qualities

The flesh is firm and white, has a delicate flavour and makes excellent eating. It is suited to all cooking methods but is best fried, grilled or lightly baked.

Citrus Baked King Tarakihi

4 MEDIUM FILLETS WITH SKIN ON
SALT
CRACKED PEPPER
25 G BUTTER
1 TSP BROWN SUGAR
1 CHILLI, SEEDED AND FINELY
  DICED
JUICE OF 2–3 MANDARINS
ZEST OF 1 MANDARIN
2 TBSP CHOPPED FRESH BASIL

- Scale and fillet the tarakihi with the skin on. Make diagonal cuts along each flank on the skin side so that the fillets won't curl when cooked. Season both sides of the fillets with a sprinkle of salt and cracked pepper to taste.
- Lay the fillets flesh side down in a greased oven dish.
- Melt the butter and sugar together and stir in chilli, juice and zest. Baste the top of each fillet with a good measure of the mix.
- Sprinkle chopped basil on top of each fillet.
- Bake in an oven preheated to 200°C for 10–15 minutes. Serve.

Bag limits

All regions no limit
Minimum size: none
Minimum set-net mesh:
100 mm

Gemfish

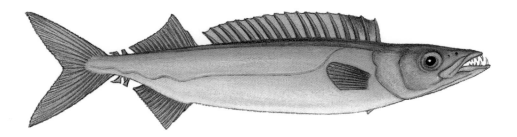

This ugly dude is sometimes mistaken for its cousin, the barracouta, which is unfortunate because it is the white sheep of the snake mackerel family. It looks like a fat barracouta, being thicker and deeper in the body and having larger eyes, and can be distinguished by its two lateral lines.

The skin is smooth, bluish along the back and silver along the flanks. The dorsal fin has a black blotch at the front. Gemfish average 60–90 cm in length but can exceed 170 cm.

Distribution

Gemfish are widespread in New Zealand waters, although dotted about in small pockets, and not especially abundant in any particular area. They have a wide depth range but are commonly sought in 150–300 m. Like barracouta, they are aggressive carnivores, feeding largely on fish and squid. They are most active from the bottom through to the middle of the water column, and are present in small numbers around areas of offshore foul.

Bag limits

All regions no limit
Minimum size: none

Hook, Line and Sinker

Gemfish are usually taken as a by-catch when other deep-water species are sought and put up a reasonable fight. A ledger rig with heavy sinker, large recurve hooks and big strip baits is the favoured method of attack. Gemfish have sharp teeth, so care is required when removing hooks.

Food Qualities

Mistakenly, many anglers toss gemfish overboard for the simple reason they look like barracouta. However, they are excellent eating, producing thick, moist fillets that are high in fat and suitable for most cooking methods. Smoking and baking are the preferred methods for dealing with this delicate-tasting fish.

Silver Warehou

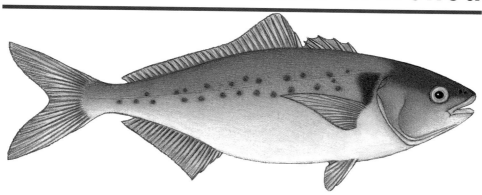

The silver warehou has a slender body, a pale-blue to silver coloration, a dark head and a lightly but distinctively pitted skin. There is a light blotch near the pectoral fin and a row of faint spots along the flanks.
Older, larger fish are slightly deeper through the body. Thought to be fast-growing, silver warehou reach some 65 cm in length and live for about eight years.

Distribution

Silver warehou are found in most New Zealand waters but are most abundant along both coasts south of Cook Strait and along the Chatham Rise. They favour depths of 200–500 m. Juveniles are common as far north as the Hauraki Gulf and also swim in shallow water. Throughout Cook Strait mature fish are regularly taken at around 60 m. Silver warehou feed mainly on plankton.

Hook, Line and Sinker

Silver warehou are best targeted midwater by drifting flasher rigs resembling planktonic creatures over pinnacles. They will also take small jigs.

Food Qualities

The flesh is firm, pinkish and high in fat. It is suited to all cooking methods but best cooked quickly over a high heat.

Bag limits

🟡 South 15
Combined finfish bag: 30
Minimum size: none
Minimum set-net mesh:
100 mm

Other regions no limit
Minimum size: none
Minimum set-net mesh:
none

Yellowfin Tuna

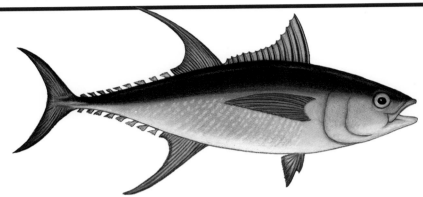

A hugely popular game fish, the yellowfin tuna is all muscle and power. Its round, streamlined body tapers sharply to a narrow crescent-shaped tail, is metallic dark blue above, often has a yellow stripe along the flank and is silvery white below.

The pectoral fins are very long, and the second dorsal fin and the anal fin are long and curved. New Zealand yellowfins average around 100 cm in length and 30 kg in weight but can grow to some 200 cm.

Distribution

Yellowfin tuna are migratory and pelagic. They visit New Zealand waters from early December to about April, depending on conditions. The main fishing grounds extend from East Cape to Northland, where yellowfins can be found throughout the thermocline.

Hook, Line and Sinker

Yellowfins are commonly taken by trolling lures but will respond to a variety of techniques. Tackle of 15–37 kg is standard. Jigging, cubing and both live and drifted baits all promise a good catch when the tuna are on. Like other tuna, yellowfins feed on small pelagic fish, often herding them into 'meatballs' before crashing through them in a feeding frenzy. Targeting meatballs is a popular method of getting on to yellowfins.

Food Qualities

The flesh has a lower oil content than that of other tuna, making it ideal for sashimi. It is darkish pink in colour and suited to baking or pan-frying over a high heat to medium or medium-rare. Overcooking dries it out and renders it similar to canned tuna.

Bag limits

All regions no limit
Minimum size: none

Yellowfin Tuna and Orange Dressing

4 LARGE YELLOWFIN TUNA STEAKS
1/2 CUP FRESH ORANGE JUICE
1 TSP HONEY
2 TBSP OLIVE OIL
2 TSP LIGHTLY ROASTED SESAME SEEDS
1 TSP WHITE-WINE VINEGAR
1 TSP SOY SAUCE
EXTRA OLIVE OIL FOR BASTING
CRACKED PEPPER

- Gently warm the orange juice in a pan and dissolve the honey in it. Add the olive oil, sesame seeds, vinegar and soy sauce, stirring well. Do not boil. Turn off the heat but keep the sauce warm.
- Baste the steaks with a coating of olive oil seasoned with cracked pepper. Grill for 3–4 minutes each side — medium to medium-rare — then leave to stand for a few minutes.
- Spoon a little sauce over each steak and serve immediately.

Albacore Tuna

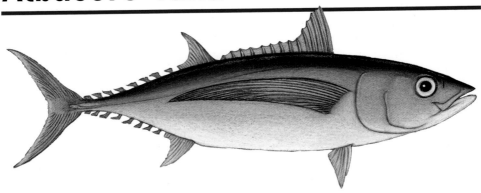

The albacore tuna is dark metallic blue along the back and has silvery-grey flanks. The pectoral fins are long, extending as far back as the anal fin. The body is deepest near the second dorsal fin, and the rear edge of the tail is white. The eyes appear large in proportion to the head and body. Average length is 50–70 cm and weight 3.5–5.5 kg.

Distribution

The albacore is a migratory pelagic species, at home in tropical to subtropical waters. It is most abundant from the Bay of Plenty to Hawke's Bay on the east coast, extending south of Kaikoura, and off Westland and New Plymouth on the west coast, reaching as far as southern Fiordland. Albacore are present in New Zealand waters throughout the year. Adults swim deep in winter, juveniles surface-swim in summer.

Hook, Line and Sinker

Albacore are top-notch sport on light tackle and will readily attack a variety of trolled lure patterns. They respond well to bullet-shaped feather or tinsel lures in various colours but snap at practically anything. They can also be taken cubing, with live baits and drifted cut baits. Albacore are schooling fish so can provide extended sport.

Food Qualities

Albacore should be bled and chilled as soon as possible after being caught. The flesh is firm and pinkish, has a medium fat content and lightens on cooking. It is suitable for sashimi, baking, frying and smoking.

The secret of cooking albacore is to treat it like steak, using plenty of heat to sear it quickly and serving it while still pink in the middle. It is best eaten fresh, rather than freezing it for later.

Pan-fried Albacore

500–800 G ALBACORE FILLETS CUT
  INTO 4 CM CUBES
1/2 CUP LIGHT SOY SAUCE
2 TBSP LEMON JUICE
GRATED ZEST OF A LEMON
1 TBSP SWEET CHILLI SAUCE
CRACKED PEPPER
DASH OF OLIVE OIL
1 TBSP BUTTER

• Combine the soy, juice, zest, chilli sauce and cracked pepper. Marinate the fish in the mixture for half an hour, turning occasionally.
• Heat a dash of olive oil and a tablespoon of butter in a pan over a high heat and quickly sear the cubes on all sides. Remove and serve hot while the flesh is still pink in the middle.

Bag limits

All regions
no limit
Minimum size: none

Black Marlin

The black marlin varies in colour along its back from dark greyish blue to brownish, which changes abruptly to white on the flanks and belly. Faint vertical stripes can sometimes be seen on freshly caught fish.

Solid and heavily built, the black averages 100–200 kg in New Zealand waters but can reach weights in excess of 450 kg. It has distinctive curved pectoral fins that are fixed and cannot be folded against the body. The first dorsal fin is lower than that of other marlins and the bill is shorter and thicker.

Distribution

The black marlin is migratory, visiting New Zealand waters from December to June. It is most common from East Cape north, although blacks have been hooked as far south as Taranaki, and sightings suggest they may extend along the west coast of the South Island. While the black marlin is an oceanic species, it favours water around islands and over foul ground, and feeds on pelagic fish and squid.

Bag limits

All regions
no limit
Minimum size: none

Hook, Line and Sinker

The black marlin is a top-rated game fish, tackle of 37 kg being required to counter its sheer power and size. It is best targeted along current lines, around headlands and over drop-offs and areas of foul. Slow-trolled live baits are most effective, but blacks will also take lures and live bait drifted under a balloon around reefs.

Food Qualities

Black marlin flesh is firm and white and suitable for grilling, baking, frying and smoking. When fresh it makes excellent sashimi.

Blue Marlin

The blue marlin is dark metallic blue along the back and upper sides, lightening to white on the underside. Pale vertical stripes may be visible on freshly caught fish. The body is rounded and stouter than that of the striped marlin.

The dark blue pectoral fin is movable and can be tucked against the body. Blue marlin average 100–200 kg in New Zealand waters but can grow to around 460 kg.

Distribution

A New Zealand visitor from January to April, the blue is likely to be found further offshore than other marlins. Its range extends as far south as East Cape, but it is more common in northern waters. Small populations extend down the west coast as far as Taranaki.

Hook, Line and Sinker

The blue is considered the most challenging of marlins to catch. Tackle of 37 kg is required to counter its speed and unpredictable fighting characteristics. It is commonly taken by trolling lures but will also take slow-trolled live baits. Trolling hookless lures to excite blues, and then switching to drifting a live bait in front of their snouts — a technique called tease and switch — is also effective.

Food Qualities

The flesh is pale and firm in texture. It makes excellent eating — smoked, grilled or baked.

Bag limits

All regions
no limit
Minimum size: none

Striped Marlin

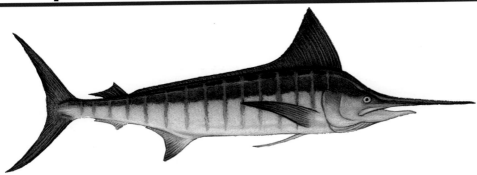

The striped marlin, distinguished by its long tapering body and flat sides, is the slender member of the marlin family. It is a rich metallic blue above, blue-grey along the flanks and white underneath.

Vertical blue to turquoise stripes slash the sides. These become more vivid when the fish is excited, and remain distinct after death.

The dorsal fin sits high and is bright blue, sometimes with darker markings. The pectoral fin is movable and can be tucked flush against the body. Striped marlin average 90–120 kg in New Zealand waters but can grow to around 200 kg. They are thought to be fast-growing and to live for about 10 years.

Distribution

Striped marlin frequent New Zealand waters from December to June, migrating to feeding grounds there from the tropical waters of the Indian and Pacific oceans.

Common haunts include the Three Kings Islands, Northland, the Bay of Islands, south to around East Cape, and all down the North Island west coast. Cook Strait was thought to mark the southern boundary of their range, but in recent years they have been caught along the west coast of the South Island.

Hook, Line and Sinker

Striped marlin are most commonly taken on surface-trolled lures in blue water off the coast. They will take slowly trolled live baits, and the tease-and-switch technique can also be productive. Surface-skipping trolled dead baits is less popular than it once was but still effective. Stripies are spectacular fighters, known for their powerful runs, leaps and tail-walking displays. Tackle of 24–37 kg is standard.

Food Qualities

The flesh is reddish pink, high in fat, firm and low in moisture, so is best suited to smoking. It also bakes well, but is quite rich and dries out easily if overcooked.

When smoked correctly, striped marlin is succulent and moist, allowing it to be frozen for 12 months or more without losing quality, provided it is vacuum packed.

Smoked Striped Marlin Pâté

250 G SMOKED STRIPED MARLIN
250 G CREAM CHEESE
2 SPRING ONIONS, FINELY
  CHOPPED
1 TBSP SWEET CHILLI SAUCE
1 CLOVE GARLIC, FINELY
  CHOPPED
JUICE OF QUARTER OF A LEMON
2 TBSP MAYONNAISE
Serves 6–8

- Blend all the ingredients in a food processor to form a paste. Spoon into a dish and refrigerate.
- This pâté will keep for a week in the fridge and can be frozen for longer-term preservation.

Bag limits

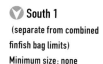 **South 1**
(separate from combined finfish bag limits)
Minimum size: none

Other regions
no limit
Minimum size: none

Kahawai

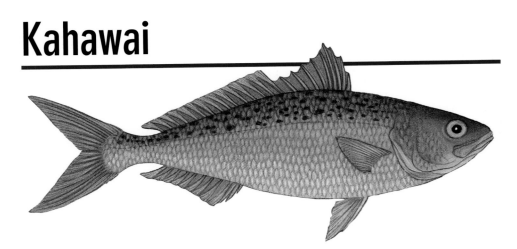

The humble kahawai is the most maligned of New Zealand fish, often being relegated to the bait bucket. Yet it has probably introduced more people to fishing than any other species, makes superb eating and, kilo for kilo, puts up a better fight than any other.

It has an elongated, streamlined body and a high front dorsal fin. It is greenish blue along the back, with irregular dark markings, and silver on the flanks and belly. Juveniles are distinguished by vertical rows of brown spots on the flanks.

Kahawai — sometimes inaccurately referred to as sea trout or sea salmon — average 40–50 cm in length and 2–4 kg in weight but can grow upwards of 70 cm and 7 kg. They grow moderately quickly and are believed to live for up to 25 years. Populations have suffered from heavy commercial fishing.

The Kermadec kahawai, a distinct species of the Far North, may weigh as much as 15 kg.

Distribution

The kahawai is pelagic, living mainly in the middle to upper water column and generally found within 50 m. Predominantly an inshore species, it is widespread throughout New Zealand coastal waters but most abundant north of Kaikoura. Kahawai cruise in shoals of similar-sized fish through a diverse range of habitats: open water, harbours, rocky coastlines, sandy beaches, estuaries and some distance upriver. They are migratory and are thought to spawn between September and early December.

Hook, Line and Sinker

The kahawai is renowned for its splendid fighting behaviour, so light tackle (4–6 kg) is usually preferred. Being one of the easiest of fish to catch, it is popular with beginners. It takes baits, preferably cut fresh fish, jigs, lures and flasher rigs. Ledger rigs, stray lines and running rigs with hook sizes of 3–6/0 cover most situations. When surface feeding, kahawai are suckers for small lures trolled some distance behind a boat. Spinning at river mouths is another popular method.

rig	hook sizes											line weight							
	1/0	2/0	3/0	4/0	5/0	6/0	8/0	10/0	12/0	13/0	14/0	2	4	6	8	10	15	24	37
Stray line					●									●	●				
Ledger rig			●	●										●	●				
Running rig					●											●			
Flasher rig				●	●									●	●				

Live Bait	Trolling	Spinning	Jigs

Food Qualities

Kahawai should be bled and chilled immediately, as deterioration is rapid. The flesh is firm with a darkish tinge but cooks white. It is succulent, with a mild-to-strong flavour. It is sensational smoked but also suits frying, baking and light grilling.

Kahawai Fish Cakes

500–800 G COOKED KAHAWAI
  FILLETS (ANY METHOD)
1 CUP POTATOES/KUMARA
  MASHED WITH SOUR CREAM
1 TSP SWEET CHILLI SAUCE
CHOPPED PARSLEY
SALT
CRACKED PEPPER
1 EGG, BEATEN
FRESH BREADCRUMBS
OIL FOR FRYING

- Flake the fish into a mixing bowl and mix in the potato, chilli sauce and parsley with salt and cracked pepper to taste.
- Roll into medium-sized cakes, dip in the egg and coat in breadcrumbs. Place in the fridge for 30 minutes to firm up.
- Panfry in moderate to hot oil until golden brown on both sides.

Bag limits

Northern, Central and Challenger 20
Combined finfish bag: 20
Minimum size: none
Minimum set-net mesh:
90 mm (Northern),
100 mm (Central and Challenger)

South 15
Combined finfish bag: 30
Minimum size: none
Minimum set-net mesh:
90 mm

Kingfish

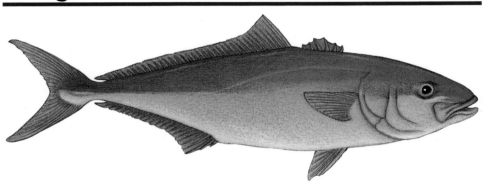

For sports fishers, the kingfish is the street-fighter of the underwater world. It has a torpedo-shaped body that tapers to a forked tail with tinges of yellow at the tips.

It is dark bluish green above, with a broad yellow band from eye to tail, and silvery white below. The first dorsal fin is small, the second tapers immediately to the tail.

Kingfish are aggressive predators and hunt in large packs. Juvenile kingfish are commonly referred to as rats. Kingies average 90–120 cm in length but can grow in excess of 150 cm and weigh over 50 kg. They are thought to be fast-growing and to live for up to 15 years.

Distribution

The kingfish is an open coastal species, broadly distributed from the upper South Island northwards, although it may be found as far south as Banks Peninsula. Being migratory, it visits inshore regions in the warmer months, frequenting harbours, estuaries and shallow bays. It is a predominantly midwater-to-surface dweller, and preys mainly on pelagic fish. Favourite haunts include offshore reefs and foul ground, especially where currents are strong, and areas around surface structures, such as buoys and moorings, and floating debris. Larger fish tend to become solitary.

Hook, Line and Sinker

Kingfish are powerful fighters so require heavy tackle — 15–37 kg. Favoured techniques are live baiting and speed jigging, but kingfish will also take surface poppers, trolled lures and even dead baits. When hooked — from either rocks or boat — kingies provide excellent sport, making long blistering runs until subdued. They are also popular with spear-fishers.

rig	hook sizes											line weight							
	1/0	2/0	3/0	4/0	5/0	6/0	8/0	10/0	12/0	13/0	14/0	2	4	6	8	10	15	24	37
Stray line					●													●	
Ledger rig					●													●	
Running rig																			
Flasher rig																			

Live Bait	Trolling	Spinning	Jigs

Food Qualities

The flesh has a darkish tinge that lightens on bleeding and cooks white. It is firm with a moderate fat content and is suited to all cooking methods. Smaller fish are often prepared as steaks.

Barbecued Kingfish Steaks

4 KINGFISH STEAKS
1/2 CUP OLIVE OIL
2 TBSP LIME JUICE
1 TBSP FRENCH MUSTARD
HANDFUL CHOPPED PARSLEY
  AND BASIL
CRACKED PEPPER TO TASTE

- Mix the oil, juice, mustard, herbs and cracked pepper to make a marinade. Put the fish in a plastic bag and pour in the marinade. Seal the bag and shake vigorously to make sure the steaks are well soused. Leave for half an hour at room temperature.
- Heat a barbecue or hot plate and grill the steaks for 3–5 minutes on each side, turning once. Drizzle a little of the marinade over the steaks as they cook.

Bag limits

All regions 3
Combined finfish bag:
5 hapuku, bass and
kingfish, with no more
than 3 kingfish
Minimum size: 65 cm
Minimum set-net mesh:
100 mm

Snapper

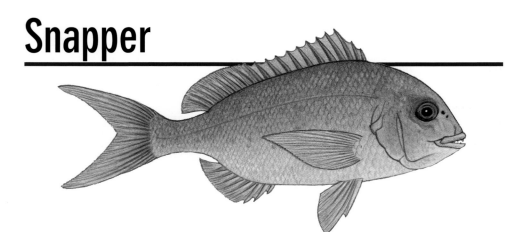

No fish has captured the imagination of recreational anglers more than the snapper. Popular because of its abundance and its distinctive head-thumping, tail-shaking runs, it is a prime target for fishers of all abilities.

The snapper is easily identified by its deep oval shape and thin body, its silvery-pink coloration darkening to copper red along the back, and a generous spattering of iridescent blue spots. Snapper are slow-growing, taking 3–5 years to reach maturity and living to over 60 years of age.

Distribution

While snapper are common throughout North Island waters, they are most abundant along the west coast and from East Cape north. The main South Island population is around the Marlborough Sounds and Tasman and Golden Bays and down the West Coast to south of Greymouth.

Snapper follow a loose pattern of migration, frequenting shallow inshore waters and estuaries from spring to late autumn and wintering offshore to depths of 150–200 m. From late spring to late summer they school in open bays to spawn. They are difficult to catch during this time.

Hook, Line and Sinker

Snapper are scavengers and opportunistic feeders, so will take a wide variety of baits from shellfish to large fish baits. But a selection of baits is advisable, as they can be fussy. Ledgers rigs are commonly used for targeting schooling snapper or when fishing deep water. Use 3–5/0 hooks, 6–10/0 for bigger fish. Lightly baited flasher rigs are also popular. Lightly weighted stray-line rigs are effective down to 30 m when fishing from the rocks or targeting large fish. In swift water or surf, try a running rig with the sinker above the trace swivel. Use 4–10 kg line, 15 kg in areas of heavy foul.

rig	hook sizes											line weight							
	1/0	2/0	3/0	4/0	5/0	6/0	8/0	10/0	12/0	13/0	14/0	2	4	6	8	10	15	24	37
Stray line						●								●		●			
Ledger rig				●	●									●		●			
Running rig				●	●											●			
Flasher rig					●									●		●			

Live Bait	Trolling	Spinning	Jigs

Food Qualities

Snapper is a popular table fish. The flesh is firm and white, breaks into large flakes and has a delicate flavour. It is suited to baking, pan-frying, grilling and smoking, but soon dries out and loses flavour when overcooked, so is best slightly underdone.

Pan-fried Snapper with Tomato and Capsicum Sauce

4 LARGE SNAPPER FILLETS
OLIVE OIL
1 ONION, FINELY DICED
1 CAN WHOLE PEELED TOMATOES
1 RED CAPSICUM, ROASTED AND PEELED
1 TBSP VINEGAR
1 TBSP CHOPPED BASIL OR ROSEMARY
CRACKED PEPPER
2 TBSP SOUR CREAM

- Heat 2 tbsp of olive oil in a saucepan and sauté the onion until soft. Add the tomatoes, capsicum, vinegar and herbs, and cook until the liquid reduces a little. Season with cracked pepper.
- Pan-fry the fillets in 2 tbsp of olive oil for 2–3 minutes each side.
- Blend the sauce well in a food processor. With the motor running, add the sour cream. Serve immediately.

Bag limits

North 15
(separate from combined finfish bag limits)
Minimum size: 27 cm
Minimum set-net mesh: 125 mm
Snapper Area 1
Bag: 9

Central 10
(separate from combined finfish bag limits)
Minimum size: 27 cm
Minimum set-net mesh: 100 mm

Challenger 10
(separate from combined finfish bag limits)
Minimum size: 25 cm
Minimum set-net mesh: 100 mm

Marlborough Sounds 3
(separate from combined finfish bag limits)

South 10
Combined finfish bag: 30
Minimum size: 25 cm
Minimum set-net mesh: 100 mm

Southern Bluefin Tuna

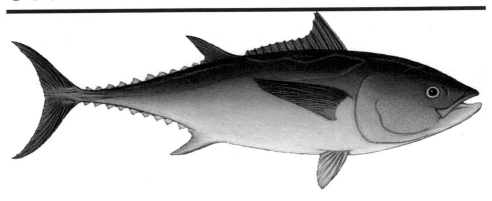

While it looks nothing like a chook, this beast is often referred to as the chicken of the sea — a reference to its taste. The bluefin is the really big-model tuna, growing up to 220 cm in length and around 200 kg in weight.

Size varies dramatically but the average weight is 30–60 kg. The body is deep and rounded, tapering to a crescent-shaped tail. It is bluish black above and silver below. The pectoral fins are short and dark bluish in colour.

Distribution

Distributed through the world's southern oceans, the bluefin is migratory and capable of moving thousands of kilometres a year. It is the most southern-ranging of the tuna and spawns along the northwest coast of Australia.

New Zealand's two main fisheries are in the northeast and on the West Coast, especially around Fiordland. There are also populations in deeper water off the East Cape, while seasonal runs occur along the west coast of the North Island. The northern season lasts from February to October, the southern from July to October. Bluefins can be found along coastal fringes as well as out in oceanic waters, and are often taken near the southern hoki grounds.

Hook, Line and Sinker

Sought after by a small percentage of hardy big-game fishers, the bluefin tuna is not to be treated lightly. Its sheer size and ballistic fighting capabilities dictate heavy gear of the order of 37 kg. Most bluefins are taken on trolled lures, while a less common but probably more effective technique is to drift deep live baits at night. Trolling lures after dark can also bring success.

Food Qualities

Premium fish fetch huge prices in Japan. The flesh is pink to red and firm and has a high fat content. It is prized as sashimi but perfectly suited to all cooking methods, although it is best undercooked because of its low moisture content. It is most commonly seared medium-rare over a high heat, and is excellent smoked.

Bag limits

All regions no limit
Minimum size: none

Barbecued Tuna with Lemon Butter

6 TUNA STEAKS WITH BONES REMOVED
CRACKED PEPPER
100 G BUTTER
$1/2$ CUP LEMON JUICE
1 TSP GRATED LEMON ZEST
1 TBSP FINELY CHOPPED SWEET BASIL OR PARSLEY

• Season steaks well on both sides with cracked pepper.
• Melt the butter and stir in the lemon juice, zest and basil or parsley.
• Cook the steaks on a hot barbecue for 3–4 minutes per side, basting with the lemon butter as you go. If it is not barbecue weather, baste the steaks and grill for a similar time.

Big-eye Tuna

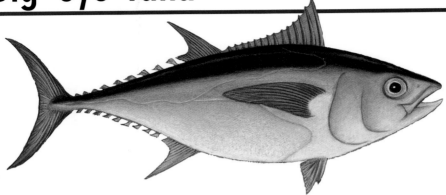

This stout member of the tuna family is similar in appearance to the albacore but much larger, reaching around 200 cm in length. In New Zealand waters average length is 100–150 cm and weight around 40 kg.

The big-eye is metallic dark blue along the back and greyish white underneath. It can be distinguished by its long pectoral fin, which extends past the second dorsal fin, and its large eyes.

Distribution

The big-eye tuna is a migratory pelagic fish common in tropical and subtropical waters. It is present throughout most of the year in offshore waters around the North Island. The main fishing grounds extend from the northeast of the North Island to well north of New Zealand. Big-eye generally swim deeper than other tuna so are not caught as frequently.

Bag limits

All regions
no limit
Minimum size: none

Hook, Line and Sinker

The most productive time to fish for big-eye is from January to March over the North Island grounds and from August to October in more northerly waters. They are generally taken as a by-catch by anglers trolling for other species in deep water but are more likely to take live baits drifted deep at night. Trolling lures at night is an increasingly popular method of targeting big-eye. Gear of 37 kg is required.

Food Qualities

With a flesh that is high in fat and superb eating, big-eye is prized in Japan as sashimi, but is also suitable for most cooking methods. It is especially nice baked, or seared and served medium to medium-rare. It is also excellent smoked.

Skipjack Tuna

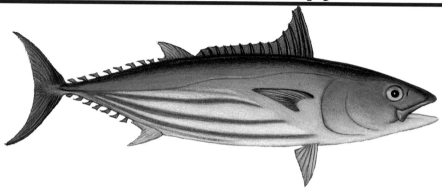

The skipjack tuna is dark purplish blue along the back and has a bluish sheen on the flanks and a silvery white belly. Four to six dark horizontal stripes run the length of the rounded, torpedo-like body.
The eyes appear large in the small conical head and the fins are small. Scales are limited to around the pectoral fins and along the lateral line.

In New Zealand waters, skipjacks are generally about 60 cm long and weigh 2–3 kg, but elsewhere they grow to over a metre in length and 10 kg in weight.

Distribution

The skipjack tuna is a migratory pelagic species found only in New Zealand's warmer waters, from Hawke's Bay and Cape Egmont north, during December–May. Skippies frequent the edge of the continental shelf at 100–400 m, where they feed predominantly on small fish and crustaceans.

Hook, Line and Sinker

These piscatorial missiles put up a good scrap on light tackle. Being pelagic, they are usually caught by game boats. They can often be seen working the surface in schools, or are given away by flocks of feeding seabirds. Trolling small lures or saltwater flies on light tackle is a common method of attack, but skippies will also take jigs or small drift baits.

Bag limits

All regions no limit
Minimum size: none

Food Qualities

Skippies deliver a dark red and very oily flesh, which breaks into large flakes. It is canned commercially and ideal for sashimi when fresh. While most anglers don't rate it as a prime species, it cooks well and is suitable for baking or searing to medium-rare over a very high heat.

Mahimahi

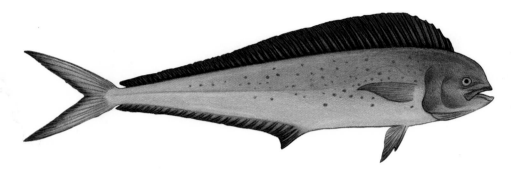

A premium table fish, the mahimahi — also known as dorado and dolphin fish — has a long body that tapers towards a sharply forked tail. It is very colourful, with metallic blues and greens along the back, golden sides with prominent spots and a white to yellow underneath.

Small specimens have pronounced vertical bars down the sides.

A high dorsal sail extends almost the length of the body, and mature males bear a prominent bony crest on the front of the head. Mahimahi are fast-growing and live for around five years. Average weight is 6–10 kg.

Distribution

The mahimahi is a subtropical pelagic species, found north of East Cape and Cape Egmont in open waters and along coastal fringes down to 85 m. It feeds on squid and a wide range of fish and plankton. Increasing numbers migrate to New Zealand waters during late December to early April.

Bag limits

All regions no limit

Minimum size: none

Minimum set-net mesh: none

Hook, Line and Sinker

Mahimahi are generally taken by trolling lures in open water along warm currents but can be caught close to shore where there is blue water. They are attracted to floating debris such as logs and weed and will take a live bait lobbed nearby. They will also attack poppers, plugs, lures and jigs cast from a boat. Tackle of 6–15 kg is usually required.

Food Qualities

Considered a premium eating fish, the flesh is creamy and firm. It is also very adaptable and suited to all cooking techniques, including the barbecue.